Pictorial History of the
AUTOMOBILE

Pictorial History of the
AUTOMOBILE

GRAHAM ROBSON

BISON GROUP

Contents

This revised edition published by
Bison Books Ltd
Kimbolton House
117A Fulham Road
London SW3 6RL
England

Copyright © 1987 Bison Books Ltd
Revised edition copyright © 1991 Bison Books Ltd

ISBN 0-86124-388-9   Printed in Hong Kong

The Dawn of Motoring

Otto, Daimler, and Benz

WHENEVER the birth of the automobile is discussed, three names stand out; all of them, Nikolaus Otto, Gottlieb Daimler and Karl Benz, were German. It was Nikolaus Otto's engine principle that made the horseless carriage practical, while it was Benz and Daimler, working independently, who first married this engine to carriages that could be driven. No matter what other chauvinistic nations – and historians – might tell you, the automobile as we know it was invented in Germany.

Otto first worked with another engineer, Eugen Langen, to develop a free-piston engine, then reorganized their company as Gasmotorenfabrik Deutz, and employed a 38-year-old engineer called Gottlieb Daimler as factory manager. It was Daimler, working sometimes with Otto and at other times on his own, who developed the four-stroke cycle to something approaching practicality. This principle was patented, but the patent was later overthrown when it was discovered that a French scientist (Beau de Rochas) had earlier postulated the theory, on paper, although he had never built an engine to prove his point.

Even at the beginning of the 1880s, when the existence of Otto's engine principle was becoming known in Germany, and when petroleum (a by-product of a process used to refine lamp oil from crude, and hitherto considered useless) was already freely available, there was still no rush to produce a viable horseless carriage.

By that time, however, Karl Benz (born near Karlsruhe in 1844) had founded Benz und Ritter (later reformed as Gasmotorenfabrik), had started building two-stroke gas engines, and was struggling to make a living. Breaking free of this, he then founded Benz und Cie and, in the winter of 1883-84 began developing his own engineering ideas, which included gasoline-powered engines.

Benz did not realize that he had a rival in Gottlieb Daimler, who had left Gasmotorenfabrik Deutz to set up shop in Bad Cannstatt (near Stuttgart) with Wilhelm Maybach, also to develop high-speed gasoline-powered engines. The two inventors went ahead in isolation, and in ignorance of each other's intentions, for the next couple of years.

As it happened, they produced their first machines at about the same time, both put them falteringly on trial at the same time, and by 1886 both had achieved some sort of reliability from their inventions. Great minds, however, did not

ABOVE RIGHT: *The four-stroke Otto engine made motor cars practical. This was the one-cylinder Daimler of 1885.*

RIGHT: *Karl Benz produced the first gasoline-engined tricycle in 1885-86.*

LEFT: *Benz's tricycle.*

think alike, for Benz's first machine was a tricycle, with two driven rear wheels, while Daimler's first engine-powered device was in fact a motorcycle, his first horseless carriage a four-wheeler.

The building of the Benz tricycle began in 1885, its first unsuccessful trial run was apparently in October of that year, and a patent relating to its design was granted in January 1886. Yet it was not until later in 1886 that it began to run properly, or to be seen around the streets of Mannheim. Its first motor show was the Paris Exhibition of 1887.

The Benz tricycle had a single-cylinder, water-cooled horizontal engine mounted amidships in the frail-looking tricycle (under the bench seat). Drive to the rear wheels was by belt, chain and a differential gear, and from a 1.0-liter capacity it produced about 0.8hp. Later a 1.7-liter 1.5hp engine was substituted, to give the little machine a viable performance.

Benz was not yet ready to put his machine on sale, even though his resourceful wife proved its reliability by taking her two teenage children for a long drive in one of the prototypes, from Mannheim to Pforzheim (62 miles) and back in 1888.

Meanwhile, in 1885 Daimler built his pioneering bicycle, which had wooden wheels and a 0.5hp 264cc single-cylinder engine. This, however, was only a try-out for the new technology, for with a certain amount of logic Daimler then decided to graft an engine into a carriage normally pulled by horses. Accordingly, he went to a local coachbuilder, bought the carriage, discarded the shafts and designed a vertical steering column instead – and set about installing an engine.

As in the Benz tricycle, the engine was mounted amidships, but not in so elegant a fashion. On the first car the 1.1hp 462cc single-cylinder engine was ahead of the line of the rear wheels, poking up through the floor of the rear passenger compartment. The Daimler also had a crude type of differential (using slipping leather discs to match the requirements of outer and inner rear wheels on corners), with final drive to the rear wheels by belts, pulleys and gears.

It was, of course, the world's first *four*-wheeler horseless carriage. Completed in 1886, it was soon to be seen journeying between Cannstatt and Unterturkheim, the latter village later to become very important to the story of the Daimler and Daimler-Benz companies.

Daimler's second car, the two-seater Stahlrad, was more logically thought out than the first, for the engine was mounted lower, under the seat and had a narrow-angle V-twin layout. Not only that, it had a four-speed transmission with a specially designed steel chassis frame.

The horseless carriage – or shall we start to call it the car? – was now a reality, but there was still a long way to go before commercial sales could begin.

98071

Cars go on Sale

Germany and France take the lead

It was in France that the motoring craze first began to spread, encouraged by the *Machines et Moteurs* and *Charronage* displays at the 1889 World's Fair in Paris. During the six months that this great exhibition was open, both Benz and Daimler engines were on show. Daimler exhibited his latest 1.6hp V-twin engined car and Emile Roger showed the most modern Benz tricycle.

Things now started to move fast. René Panhard and Emile Levassor began manufacturing Daimler engines, supplying three early examples to another French manufacturer, Armand Peugeot, and both of them decided to start building cars. By the early 1890s, therefore, a fledgling industry was beginning to take shape.

Benz, the tricycle pioneer, concentrated on selling stationary engines for a time, sold a few tricycles through Emile Roger in France, and did not build his first four-wheeler, the Viktoria, until 1893. This was a great success, with 45 built and sold in the first year, and (along with the smaller-engined Velo derivative) no fewer than 572 machines were built in 1899. At that moment, Benz was dominant in the new automobile industry.

WHEN Benz and Daimler built the world's first gasoline-powered automobiles in Germany, the law made it almost impossible for them to be driven properly. In Baden province, where the Benz was produced, the speed limit in towns was 4mph, in the country 8mph. In some parts of Germany it was quite illegal for such machines to be used on the public highway at all.

Nevertheless, some progress was made. Daimler supplied a machine for taxicab use at Stuttgart station in 1888, and a fire engine soon followed. In 1887 Daimler negotiated the French manufacturing rights to Edouard Sarazin (a Belgian), who turned to the small company of Panhard et Levassor to make the engines for him. Benz, on the other hand, was not yet ready to start selling in Germany, the first concession and deliveries going to Emile Roger's business in Paris.

The problem was, of course, that without a demand from customers, there could be no industry, and without an industry there could be no deliveries to customers. Catch 22? Yes — except that the phrase had yet to be invented. . .

ABOVE RIGHT: *This belt-driven Daimler of 1892 had a twin-cylinder engine under the body; its styling is clearly derived from that of a horse-drawn carriage. With a 2.5hp engine this car could achieve 12mph.*

RIGHT: *It took time for motoring pioneers to agree on the ideal layout for a car. Here is the Hon. CS Rolls 'driving' his 1897 Leon Bollée tricycle, with the passenger ahead of him.*

LEFT: *Daimler's first car was obviously a 'horseless carriage', with the single-cylinder engine mounted amidships ahead of the rear seat, and with a vertical steering column.*

ABOVE: *Lanchester was one of the successful British pioneers, utilising advanced technical features. This car dates from 1901.*

LEFT: *The anatomy of early motor cars laid bare – this is an 1897 Benz, showing the rear-mounted engine, and chain drive system.*

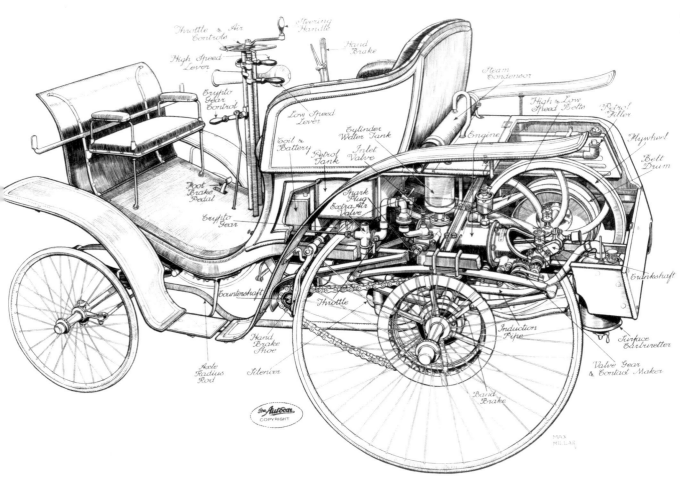

OPPOSITE ABOVE: *De Dion of France soon started building cars in numbers – this was a 1902 Motorette model.*

OPPOSITE: *Panhard's contribution to motoring was to locate the engine up front with rear-wheel-drive – a 1900 model.*

All the flavor of Edwardian motoring – British tourists in France in 1904, using a 24hp Fiat.

Daimler progress was held back by a dispute between Daimler and Maybach on one side and their co-directors on the other. It all turned sour: Daimler and Maybach set up shop on their own for a time and did not make their peace again until 1895. By this time, however, Daimler patents were not only licensed in mainland Europe, but also in the British Empire. Frederick Simms acquired them at first, but he did not proceed seriously with manufacturing plans. Instead, he sold out to a syndicate headed by Harry Lawson, who started production in Coventry in 1896.

Panhard-Levassor's first-ever car was built at the end of 1890 and became reliable in 1891 (when Panhard completed a Paris-Normandy trip of 140 miles in two days). This, however, was a mid-engined device, and it was Emile Levassor's decision to design a completely different car, with an engine at the front and drive to the rear wheels, which really set the world's automobile industry on the right path. The *système Panhard*, as it became known, placed its transmission behind the engine, and had final drive by twin side chains. It was at once practical, economical and easy to build. From late 1891, Panhards of this type went on sale, and the company did not look back. (There was nothing new about this layout, by the way, which had first been seen on Bollée's La Mancelle steam vehicle of 1878.)

Peugeot's first horseless carriage prototype had been a Serpollet-engined steam-powered device, also shown at the World's Fair in 1889, but it was during that fair that Armand Peugeot decided to use Panhard-built, Daimler-licensed gasoline engines. The first such Peugeot, built in 1890, had a bicycle-type tubular steel frame and was really a refined version of the mid-engined Daimler Stahlrad design, although fitted with transverse leaf-spring front suspension. The first hand-built Peugeots were delivered in 1891 and sales in numbers began soon afterwards.

At this point in history, the world's automobile industry consisted of just four manufacturers – Benz, Daimler, Panhard-Levassor and Peugeot – with its center of gravity still in the German engines of Benz and Daimler. Other countries – the United States, Britain and Italy among them – were waiting in the wings, but for the moment the glory belonged to France and, above all, Germany.

But not for long. The industrial might of the United States was about to join in.

Pioneers in the New World

America gets in on the act

IN the 1880s and 1890s, the world was still a large place, so it took a little time for the fame of Benz and Daimler to float across the Atlantic to the United States. However, once this young, vigorous and technically ambitious nation got involved in the development of cars, progress was extremely rapid.

The very first American motor vehicle seems to have been the steam-powered Schank tricycle, which was shown at the Ohio State Fair in 1886. This was quite impractical (the engine was reputed to have been as 'large as a kitchen stove'), but at least it inspired a cycle manufacturer called Charles Duryea to start experiments of his own.

By 1891 the New York piano-maker William Steinway had secured American patent rights from Gottlieb Daimler, but he took time to set up a factory on Long Island, and then mainly made stationary and marine engines. The first successful American car was a three-wheeler designed by John W Lambert of Ohio City, which was demonstrated early in 1891, though never developed. In the same year Henry and Philip Nadig of Allentown, Pennsylvania, produced a single-cylinder four-wheeler, two years later substituted a two-cylinder engine, and ran the car until 1903.

Neither of these cars, however, went into production. The honor of being America's first domestically designed production car went to the Duryea of 1895. The first Duryea prototype of 1893, which was built at Springfield, Massachusetts, was really a converted horse buggy with a single-cylinder engine, had friction drive and was a failure. The

TOP: *North America's first production car was the Duryea, built in Springfield from 1895. This very early example (dating from 1896) has tiller steering and is about as simple as a car can be.*

LEFT: *This 1902 Cadillac helped found the reputation of one of the world's great marques. In the next few years the Cadillac got bigger, faster, and more grand.*

definitive production car of 1895 had a 1¾ hp twin-cylinder engine with a three-speed transmission and an unsprung rear axle. It was much more successful and sales began at once.

At this point a New York solicitor, George Baldwin Selden, published his original patent application of 1879 (why had it taken him 16 years to get round to it?), which defined a 'reliable road locomotive' with an engine 'of the compression type' in rather vague terms. Although he had not actually built a prototype to prove his principle, on these grounds he claimed that all gasoline-driven vehicles developed since then infringed his patents, and that according to United States law these patents would hold for the next 17 years. He did not immediately try to enforce these claims. Most nascent United States car-makers, in fact, did not even know that they might be transgressing a patent.

The 'Selden Patent' only became public knowledge, and was enforced, after a company which became the Electric Vehicle Company (EVC) took up the patents, and in 1902 began to enforce a royalty through the newly formed Association of Licensed Automobile Manufacturers (ALAM). If the

stubborn Henry Ford had not decided to challenge this patent, Selden, the EVC and the ALAM might all have been receiving a fat income for life. As it was, Ford fought the patent through court after court, finally winning his case in 1911.

Before the end of the 1890s, however, more and more American car companies had been founded, and in 1899 it was estimated that 57 companies employed 2241 people. Five years later, as the popularity of the automobile mushroomed, there were 178 companies and more then 12,000 workers. About 50 American-built cars existed by 1900, but within a year there were 4192 on the still-awful roads, and by 1905 this figure had rocketed to 24,250. Consider these famous names:

Ransom Olds began playing around with steam and electric cars, saying that he 'couldn't stand the smell of horses,' but his first gasoline-driven car was the legendary Curved Dash Oldsmobile, which went on sale in 1901. This stubby little creation had a water-cooled engine lying amidships under the floor and longitudinal leaf springs connecting front and rear axles. By 1905, 36 cars a day were being

OPPOSITE: *At its height, Packard was one of the USA's most important auto makers, although it all started modestly, with models like this 1900 example.*

RIGHT: *One of America's memorable early cars, the famous 'curved dash' Oldsmobile.*

BELOW: *By 1908 Packard had become larger and more grand; already this was one of the more patrician American makes.*

BELOW: *By 1910 American cars were taking on a distinctive style – this being an Oldsmobile.*

BOTTOM *A famous, if not a significant Ford: an 1896 Quadricycle, with Henry at the wheel.*

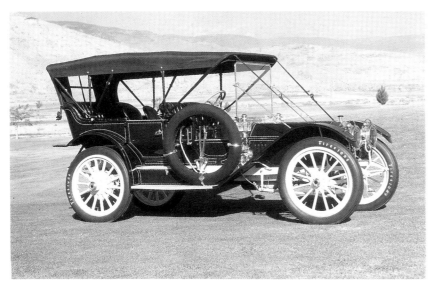

produced at the Lansing, Michigan, factory. Oldsmobile became a member of the General Motors Corporation a few years later.

Alexander Winton was a Cleveland bicycle-maker who built his first experimental car in 1897 and started selling two-cylinder cars in 1898. Among the earliest Winton customers were the Packard brothers, and it is said that Winton's attitude to complaints led to the Packards setting up their own business.

JW and WD Packard set up shop at Warren, Ohio, in 1899, and their first car was a single-cylinder 12hp model. This was soon supplanted by faster and more powerful versions, and in 1903 one of the latest cars was driven from San Francisco to New York in 61 days. Packard moved to Detroit in 1903 and remained an independent concern until 1954.

I should also mention bathtub-maker David Buick's first car of 1903, the original Cadillac of 1903, and the Rambler, built by the Jefferys family from 1902. Plus, of course, Ford.

Ford's impact on the American way of life was so enormous that a separate section is devoted to the company's growth (*see* page 51).

FIRST · CAR

The Best Car in the World

Rolls-Royce or Cadillac?

T HERE are some conundrums that defy analysis. Facts are facts and can be displayed, but opinions can only be justified by emotion and passion. Here is a perennial riddle — what is, or was, the Best Car in the World?

British enthusiasts have no doubt, but Germans would disagree. As for the Americans — one of the easiest ways to start an argument with them is to suggest that Rolls-Royce have *always* built the best cars in the world, and that Cadillac, Lincoln or Duesenberg do not figure.

Even in the early 1900s, when the art and science of building cars was developing so precariously, a few types of car stood out from the common herd. By 1910 the well-to-do knew where they should be buying their cars. By 1920 the list was well established, and nothing that has happened since 1930 has changed that.

In Britain, the best of the best was undoubtedly Rolls-Royce. In Germany it was Mercedes. In the United States it was Cadillac. If Mercedes (later Mercedes-Benz) had not then gone for the sporting market instead of the custom of the 'carriage trade', they might always have been rivals for the crown; in the event, it was not until the 1960s that they came back with a real challenger.

Rolls-Royce, in fact, was born out of Henry Royce's dissatisfaction with a French Decauville which he ran for a short time. The Manchester-based electrical engineer who designed and developed better cars, joined up in a marketing

TOP: *Only a marque like Cadillac, so sure of its reputation, would call this interesting 1910 model a 'Runabout.'*

ABOVE: *The Alpine Eagle version of the Rolls-Royce 40/50hp model, participating in a 1914 alpine trial.*

arrangement with the Hon. Charles Rolls, and began to evolve the Rolls-Royce marque. Royce was happy to let high-class coachbuilders produce bodywork for these cars; the Manchester and (later) the Derby factories only produced Rolls-Royce rolling chassis.

The first of the truly great Rolls-Royces was the 40/50hp model (also colloquially known as the 'Silver Ghost'), an expensive and magnificently detailed 7.0-liter (later 7.4-liter) six-cylinder machine whose basic design was to run through until 1925. The 'Ghost' nickname, incidentally, was applied after the quietness and refinement of the splendid engine became apparent.

For many years, a Rolls-Royce chassis was designed and built almost without regard to cost. Royce the perfectionist knew only one way to design anything – the best way – and if this was expensive it had to be accepted. For that reason it always took a long time for the latest technical trends to be accepted – just in case the trend was only a craze – and the well-proven solution to a problem was always preferred to the latest gimmick.

On the other hand, Royce and his successors were always happy to go out and buy the rights to a new component (or copy a good idea!) if it seemed suitable for Rolls-Royce cars. In the 1920s the Hispano-Suiza mechanical brake servo was used, while in the 1930s the new-fangled General Motors synchromesh soon put in an appearance. Later in the decade, the company's first independent front suspension layout was apparently based on that used by the American Packard concern.

LEFT: *Full pre-war magnificence expressed in this 1912 Rolls-Royce 40/50hp model.*

BELOW: *The Rolls-Royce 'Alpine Eagle' of 1913, a real sports car.*

OPPOSITE: *A USA-built Springfield Rolls-Royce of 1926.*

OPPOSITE BELOW: *So typical of early 1920s American styling – the 1920 Cadillac 59 Victoria.*

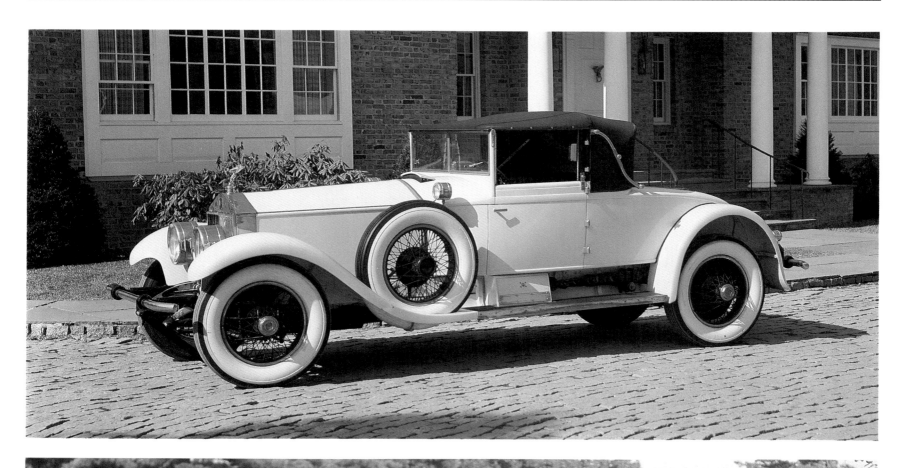

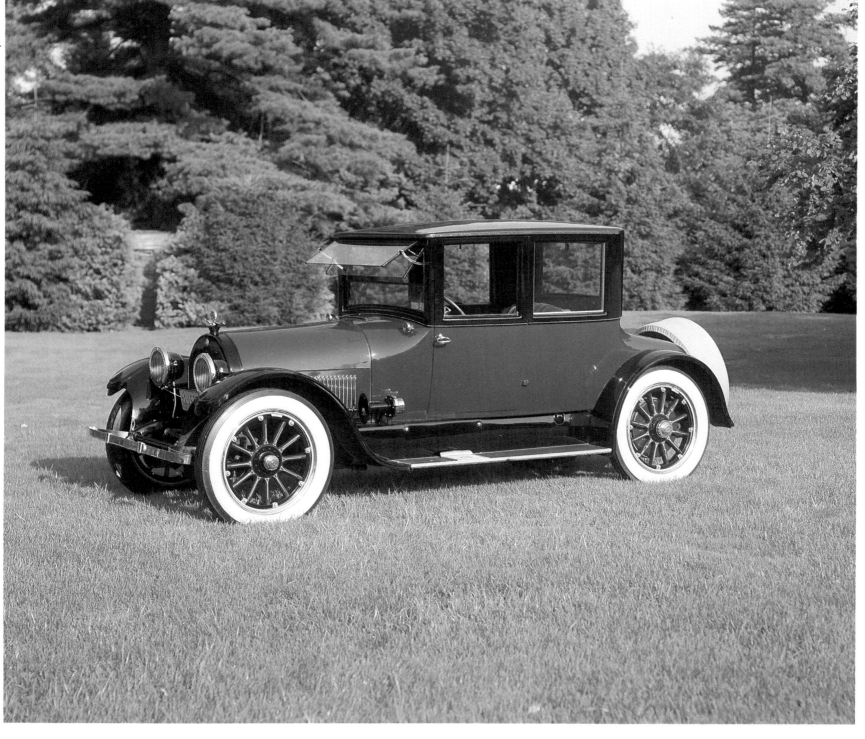

To supplement the 40/50hp, Rolls-Royce produced the 3.1-liter 20hp model from 1922, and in 1925 the original 40/50hp was displaced by the 7.7-liter engined New Phantom (also known as Phantom I). For the next 10 years both types were gradually improved – 20hp becoming 20/25, then 25/30, and finally Wraith, New Phantom becoming Phantom II – until, in 1935, came the most complex Rolls-Royce so far, the 7.3-liter engined V12 Phantom III. By 1939, however, much of the Rolls-Royce business was concentrated on the building of aircraft engines (including the magnificent V12 Merlin unit), and cars were almost an irrelevance.

From 1921 to 1931, the 40/50hp and later the New Phantom chassis were also manufactured in the United States, at Springfield, Massachusetts, and were graced with sumptuous American-built coachwork. The effects of the Depression finally put paid to what was never a profitable venture.

The name 'Cadillac' came from the French army officer, Antoine de la Mothe Cadillac, who founded the city of Detroit in 1701. It was William Murphy who adopted this name when setting up his new car company, in Detroit, in 1902. He got Henry M Leland to design his new car for him. Cadillac's motto : 'Craftsmanship a creed, accuracy a law,' stems from those early days and, in spite of the styling excesses committed in its name in later years, it was usually adhered to.

The first Cadillac was a single-cylinder four-seater tourer, and it was the Model K version of this design which added the name Cadillac to the automobile hall of fame. In Britain, to prove Cadillac's ideas about precision manufacture and interchangeability of parts, three cars were completely stripped out, the parts mixed up, then reassembled in no particular way, run for 500 miles at the Brooklands race track, and encountered no problems at all.

Cadillac's growing reputation led to the company being absorbed into the new General Motors combine in 1909, and it was under General Motors ownership that the first Cadillac V8 was introduced in 1915. During the 1920s, Cadillacs usually looked conventional (some say undistinguished), but always had impeccably engineered chassis. While Rolls-

FAR LEFT: *The Rolls-Royce 40/50hp, or 'Silver Ghost,' was built until the mid-1920s. This is one of the last, produced in 1925.*

LEFT: *If Rolls-Royce could have its Spirit of Ecstasy, so could Cadillac! This is the V16 radiator mascot of 1931.*

ABOVE: *Cadillac's most complex and expensive between-wars car was the V16 model, launched in 1930 and soon joined by a V12 version. Rolls-Royce did not match such enterprise until 1935.*

Royce were only building 1000 cars a year, Cadillac produced 47,420 in 1927.

Cadillac introduced the electric self-starter, the generator, even the high-tension electrical system named after its inventor, GM's 'Boss' Kettering. In 1928 there was not only a new V8 engine, but the world's first use of synchromesh transmission. Vacuum-boosted brakes were provided from 1932 and independent front suspension soon followed.

Cadillac's most startling innovations of the 1930s, however, were the 165hp 7.4-liter 45-degree V16 engine of 1930, which appeared at the beginning of the Depression, and the closely related V12 which followed it. From 1941, too, there was the world's first fully automatic transmission as an option. The adoption of the Cadillac motto 'Standard of the World,' is hardly a surprise.

But, which was the Best Car in the World? I leave you to argue it out.

Motoring for the Masses

The rise of Ford, and General Motors

FOR the first 20 years or so the automobile tended to be the rich man's plaything, built in small numbers by craftsmen in small factories, with the very minimum of mechanization and tooling. It was not until North American entrepreneurs got their teeth into the problem, realizing the potential of 'wheels for the world,' that the automobile began to reach the mass market.

Right from the start, Detroit emerged as the center of North America's automobile industry, though it was not until the late 1900s that the large companies began to appear. Until then, cars like Oldsmobile, Buick, and Ford were separately built, in larger quantities than those being produced in Europe at that time, but still not in the huge numbers that were to become standard.

For the Americans, motoring for the masses gradually evolved between 1900 and 1910, when two large concerns began to emerge – Ford and General Motors. Then, as now, they were the most important influences on any other car-maker in the country. The only difference between Detroit in the 1910s and 1920s and the Detroit of today is that Ford was then substantially larger than General Motors.

Henry Ford came from a farming family, but he gravitated to Detroit in the 1890s (before an automobile industry had been set up), was fascinated by engineering, and began working for the Edison Illuminating Company. For his own interest, Henry Ford built the Quadricycle prototype in 1896, but it was not until he set up the Detroit Automobile Company (DAC) that he began to sell cars to the public.

Like many such small firms, DAC failed, so the 38-year-old Ford had to start again, this time with the Henry Ford Company and, shortly, with the Ford Motor Co. Ltd in 1903. That family-owned company then set down roots, and grew and grew, until it became the biggest car-making complex in the world. The initial capitalization was $28,000 and the first cars cost $850. Success was swift, for within a year vast profits were being made and almost $100,000 was paid out in dividends.

The first production Ford was the Model A, but it was the Model T, announced in 1908, that really rocketed the company to worldwide fame. To make more and more of these cars, the massive Highland Park factory was built, assembly plants were opened in other countries, then after World War I the River Rouge 'greenfield' site was developed; that

OPPOSITE: *After building more than 15 million Model Ts, Ford produced the all-new, very different Model A in 1927.*

BELOW: *Buick was one of the founder members of the General Motors group. This car, a 10E model, was produced in 1909.*

ABOVE: *A Model T Ford, one of the 15 million built between 1908 and 1927. This particular car dates from 1916, and at that stage the Model T still had no front wheel brakes. Model T styling changed only slowly over the years and the famous radiator style was always retained.*

LEFT: *Walter Chrysler, formerly of Buick and Willys, set up his own business in 1923, and soon had a fine reputation. Before long Chrysler was the third most important grouping in the USA. This was a 1927 Tourer.*

OPPOSITE: *Chrysler's first production car was the six-cylinder engined '70.' This is the Model B Phaeton of 1924.*

factory is still the pivot of Ford's United States assembly today.

Along the way Henry Ford controlled his company and its thousands of workers in a very paternal way. He introduced the $5-day at a time when most Detroit car-makers paid $2, he refused to allow unions in his factories until the late 1930s, and he refused to see a Model T successor developed until 1927, when it was almost too late. That was the moment when General Motors took over market leadership, which they have never relinquished.

General Motors was founded in 1908 by the wheeler-dealing William C Durant, who had been in control of Buick since 1904. By 1907 Buick was selling 8800 cars a year, second only to Ford's total of 10,200, having come up from nothing five years earlier. One of its rivals was Cadillac, a company that had been building cars since 1903. Another competitor, Oldsmobile, was one of the United States' car-making pioneers with prototypes on the road in 1896. Its small 'curved-dash' model made it one of America's most notable car-making companies in the early 1900s. Durant masterminded a merger between Buick, Cadillac and Oldsmobile to form General Motors. Ford might also have been included, but the irascible Henry could not stomach such a deal.

At that stage, what is now General Motors' largest nameplate, the Chevrolet, had not even come into existence. In 1910, in a complex financial situation, GM's bankers ousted Durant from the chair, whereupon he went off with racing driver Louis Chevrolet and developed the new Chevrolet road car. Eventually Durant bought his way back into control of General Motors in 1915, but he did not add the Chevrolet marque to the group until 1918.

Other cars, such as Oakland, Sheridan and Scripps-Booth, were also manufactured under the General Motors umbrella, but the group remained a corporate shambles until Alfred P Sloan became executive vice-president in 1921. In the next years, Sloan transformed the agglomerate into a much more logical group, sales rose, costs fell, and General Motors began to challenge Ford for automobile industry leadership. The British car company Vauxhall was taken over in 1925 (General Motors also talked to Austin, but did not finalize a deal), and the German company Opel was absorbed in 1928. Pontiac grew out of Oakland in 1926 and replaced it completely from 1931.

By the 1930s, Chevrolet was the fastest-selling car in the United States with Oldsmobile, Pontiac and Buick all well established in the 'top ten' league table. Not only that, but Cadillac still set high standards for quality and engineering, and was one of America's very best cars. General Motors' cars were being built in factories spread all around the United States – the corporation was in a dominant position, one it would maintain over the decades to come, in spite of the Industry's fluctuating fortunes.

Motoring for Fun

The birth of the sports car

THE early progress of automobile design can easily be summarized: in the 1880s engineers struggled to make automobiles go at all, in the 1890s they made them go reliably, and in the 1900s they made them go beautifully. But it was not until the machines had proved they were reliable – and at the same time predictable – that they could be used for pleasure.

What is a sports car? There is no easy description. In the 1900s, however, it would be true to say that most pioneer drivers were also sportsmen – they had to be, to put up with the discomforts that the driving of the period entailed. Perhaps it is simplest to suggest that a car which could be used for fun was, automatically, a sports car.

In the beginning, to use a high-performance car on near-deserted roads must have been sheer heaven. Or was it? If those roads were not in poor condition, or plagued by dust, and if there were no punctures to be mended, if there was no need to search desperately for gasoline, and no need to look around for repairs, perhaps it was. . .

In Britain, too, there was the problem of the overall open-road speed limit of 12mph before 1904 and 20mph thereafter. This was ruthlessly and rigidly enforced by the police, and the local magistrates were often viciously anti-driver in their judgment.

LEFT: *Early sports cars in the German Prince Henry Trials of 1908. Even though this photograph is 80 years old, the sports car 'line' is already obvious.*

RIGHT: *A very early example of a Bugatti – the Type 10 of 1908. Bugatti was to be in the forefront of auto design for the next 30 years.*

BELOW: *Several American manufacturers took up the fashionable 'raceabout' style in the 1910s – this being the well-known Mercer marque.*

ABOVE: *This Amilcar Type CO of 1926 was one of several French sports cars which starred in the 1920s, then faded rapidly away.*

LEFT: *The MG M-Type Midget of 1929/30.*

RIGHT: *A between-wars Frazer Nash.*

Nowadays we might think of a typical sports car as a Corvette, an MG MGA or a Porsche 356 – all cars with smallish engines, compact packaging and agile road behavior. In the years before World War I, however, a sports car – in other words, a car for sporting use – was very different from that. The cars that set the trend were those massive-engined two-seaters used in the town-to-town races, in the Gordon Bennett races, and in the first British Tourist Trophy events. Mostly these were rakish models looking, sounding and going a lot faster than their 'touring' equivalents.

The very fast Mercedes car, the 1901 35hp model which dominated proceedings at the Nice Speed Week in 1901, was one such, and it inspired a rush of imitators in the next few years. The Mercedes, like its rivals from Panhard, Mors and De Dietrich, had a big and lusty four-cyclinder engine. It was only after Napier made the layout fashionable that six-cylinder cars also came along.

At that point in history, too, even companies like British Daimler and Rolls-Royce produced fast sporting machines, and with cars like the big 70hp Thomas Flyers, the Italas and the Métallurgiques also available, there was no lack of choice. But only, please note, for the wealthy.

Until about 1906 or 1907 there was really very little difference between a fast sports car and pure racing car, but once the French introduced Grand Prix racing and countries like Germany began promoting long open-road races or trials for road cars, the two types moved steadily apart. Indeed, the one event that saw the birth of the definitive two-seater sports car was the 1907 *Kaiserpreis* race, which was a four 70-mile lap event in the Taunus mountains of Germany. It was a race won by Felice Nazzaro's Fiat, but there was also much competition from Benz and Daimler.

After the last of the three Herkomer events was held in Bavaria, Prince Henry of Prussia sponsored a new series of trials to replace it. In 1908, and starting from Berlin, the first such contest saw specially designed 'Prince Henry' models developed. Within two years, Ferdinand Porsche had designed a Prince Henry Austro-Daimler, and shortly afterwards Laurence H Pomeroy also designed a Prince Henry Vauxhall for the same purpose.

Meanwhile, in the United States, American manufacturers developed the *Kaiserpreis* style of car a stage further, into what we now know as characteristic 'raceabout' models.

Of the many imitators of this fashion, some of the best known came from Locomobile (the Model H of 1905-09), Lozier (Type I), Mercer (the Raceabout) and Stutz (the Bearcat). This type of car stayed in vogue until the mid-1910s.

The definition of the sports car was now changing, to accommodate smaller, lighter and altogether more nimble two-seaters. From France in 1910 came the first of the series-production Bugattis, the Type 13 (later known as the Brescia), from Spain in 1911 the nicely detailed 3.6-liter Hispano-Suiza Alfonso model, and from Britain the 4.5-liter Talbot 25/50 model of 1914. Even the prototype Aston Martin was on the road before World War I, though sales did not begin until 1921.

In the 1920s, of course, sports cars became more and more popular, their sales increasing as fast as their size, bulk and prices fell. Not only did Bentley begin building their massive race-winning creations, but firms like Amilcar, Chenard-Walcker, Salmson and Delage of France, Alvis, Invicta, GN and Frazer Nash of Britain, Alfa Romeo and Lancia of Italy, all joined in. It was a wondrous sporting decade which established the sports car pedigree for all time.

Whatever Happened to. . .?

The cars which lost their way

One distinguished American automobile historian, Beverley Rae Kimes, once noted that there were thousands of American makes of car which had not survived to the present day. However, what is surprising is that some of the most famous names also died away in the years between the wars.

Consider the first four makes of car to be put on sale – Benz, Daimler, Panhard et Lavassor and Peugeot. The last German Daimler was built in 1902, just a year after the new Mercedes marque was adopted. Benz disappeared in favour of the Mercedes-Benz. Panhard et Levassor became Panhard almost at once, was taken over by Citroën in 1964, and breathed its last in 1967. Only Peugeot, now the dominant member of the Peugeot-Citroën-Talbot combine, has survived to the present day.

Even some of the biggest names in North America – those included in the General Motors and Chrysler combines of the 1920s and 1930s – also disappeared. One early name in General Motors was that of Oakland, a company which gave birth to Pontiac, but was eventually supplanted by its offspring. General Motors also invented the La Salle in 1927, as a cheaper type of Cadillac, but this too disappeared in 1940.

The original Chrysler group included the Maxwell, which dated from 1904, but it vanished in 1925. Not at all dismayed, Chrysler then invented De Soto in 1928, as a rather cheaper model, and this soldiered on until 1960.

Every marque which died had a different reason for doing so. In the case of Bentley, the firm set up by WO Bentley after

DO you remember Duesenberg, Cord and Auburn? Do you recall De Dion, Sunbeam and Delage? Whatever happened to the *real* Bentley? To Darracq and to Marmon? It's all very sad – between the two World Wars, some of the great names of the earlier years of the automobile disappeared. But why, and how?

RIGHT: *Duesenberg was launched in 1920 but died in 1937. killed by the Depression. This 1925 Model A was an early 'classic.'*

OPPOSITE BELOW: *The supercharged 4½-liter Bentley was the most famous of these 'vintage' models. Rolls-Royce bought the name in 1931.*

BELOW: *In the 1920s Lanchester built excellent cars. These are 40hp models of 1924 and 1925.*

OPPOSITE ABOVE: *Franklin built air-cooled cars from 1901 to 1934, but the public finally rejected them. This touring model dates from 1927.*

OPPOSITE: *There is no trace of air-cooling in this 1928 Type 12B Franklin Victoria*

Brougham. In the end, there was no advantage over water-cooled cars.

ABOVE: *Only two different Cord types were produced. This was the original 1929 L29 model, with straight-eight Lycoming engine and front-wheel-drive.*

World War I, the cars were always of the highest quality, reliability and performance, but buyers for these expensive machines were hard to find. The company overindulged in the expense of racing and finally ran out of money in 1931 when the Depression was at its worst. Rolls-Royce took over the name, but the company was never the same again.

Sunbeam was another British marque whose finest years were in the 1910s and 1920s. The first cars had been sold in 1901, and the great years began in 1909 when Louis Coatalen joined as chief designer. Sunbeams raced with success before World War I, provided reliable staff car transport on the Western Front, and became splendid sporting cars in the 1920s. In the 1930s the marque was dragged down by the Sunbeam-Talbot-Darracq (STD) combine's financial problems, and was taken over in receivership by Rootes in 1935.

The same fate befell Talbot, which had begun production in West London in 1903. Georges Roesch produced the six-cylinder 14/45hp in the mid-1920s and developed the design into the successful 75, 90 and 105 models in the early 1930s. By 1935 the Talbot was one of Britain's very finest cars, but the company was then laid low in the same way as Sunbeam, and Rootes bought up the corpse. One of the original French pioneers, De Dion, had a distinguished history before World War I; at one time or another, 140 other makes of car were using De Dion engines and other companies were copying

from the same design. After the war, however, fortunes declined and demand dropped, with the last cars being built in 1932. Darracq, another French pioneer, prospered until 1920, after which it joined forces with Sunbeam and Talbot, the name soon disappearing into the maw of the STD group.

Delage was a great manufacturer of the inter-war years, which not only prepared a whole range of fine, fast, *grand routier* models, but produced some outstanding Grand Prix racing cars. But the founder, Louis Delage, ran out of money in the mid-1930s as sales declined and was forced to sell out to Delahaye.

Amilcar was another French company that deserved better luck. Founded in 1921, Amilcar built a series of light and efficient sporting *voiturettes* with four-cylinder, six-cylinder and eight-cylinder engines. The Depression hit France just as hard as elsewhere, Amilcar's sales dropped away, and the last was built in 1939.

Several other famous American names did not make it into modern times, usually because their models became too expensive to sell in the Depression-hit United States. Consider Duesenberg of Indianapolis, whose name had already been made by racing before the first car was sold in 1920. The cars were always large, complex and expensive, not least the famous Model J and Model SJ eight-cylinder cars of 1928 and 1932, which were phenomenally powerful (the SJ had 320 hp). Although Duesenberg staggered on through the Depression, the company's partner Cord finally pulled them into bankruptcy.

Auburn came into existence in 1900 and built many fine cars before being taken over by EL Cord in 1924. Under his leadership larger and faster Auburns were produced, the Duesenberg company was bought up in 1928, and eight-cylinder and V12 models were announced in the early 1930s. The most amazing Auburn of all was the supercharged eight-cylinder Speedster Type 851 of 1935, with a guaranteed top speed of 100mph. But it all went very wrong in 1937 and the marque folded, another victim of the Depression.

The Cord was an offshoot of the Auburn and Duesenberg combine, with a supercharged front-wheel drive, eight-cylinder car, the L-29, in 1929 and a Duesenberg-inspired car, the front-wheel-drive Model 810, in 1935. The problem was that these cars were both expensive and unfamiliar to American buyers. Cord died along with Auburn and Duesenberg in 1937.

Companies come and companies go. . .

BELOW: *Delage of France built some fine Grand Touring cars in the 1920s and 1930s. This 1934 D8-15S had an eight-cylinder engine, and near-100mph top speed.*

RIGHT: *The Invicta was a typical British 'vintage' car, made only between 1925 and 1935. This 4½-liter S was a successful sports car.*

Ford's Model T

A car 'for the man in the street'

ALTHOUGH Henry Ford built his very first car, the Quadricycle, in 1896, it was not until 1908 that his still-small company launched the Model T. This not only transformed the Ford company, but completely changed the face of transportation in the United States. Between 1908 and 1927 more than 15 million Model Ts were produced, setting a record that stood for more than 40 years.

Ford's original cars, like the four-cylinder Model B of 1904 and the six-cylinder Model K that followed it, were expensive, but Henry Ford always had a dream of selling masses of cars at low prices to the 'man in the street.' It needed a disagreement with his co-directors, and the buying out of several of them, before Henry got his way. The Model T, priced at $850, was eventually launched on 1 October 1908.

BELOW: *Almost single-handed, the Model T Ford turned motoring from a rich man's hobby to everyday transport. At its height more than two million Model T Fords were built in the space of a single year.*

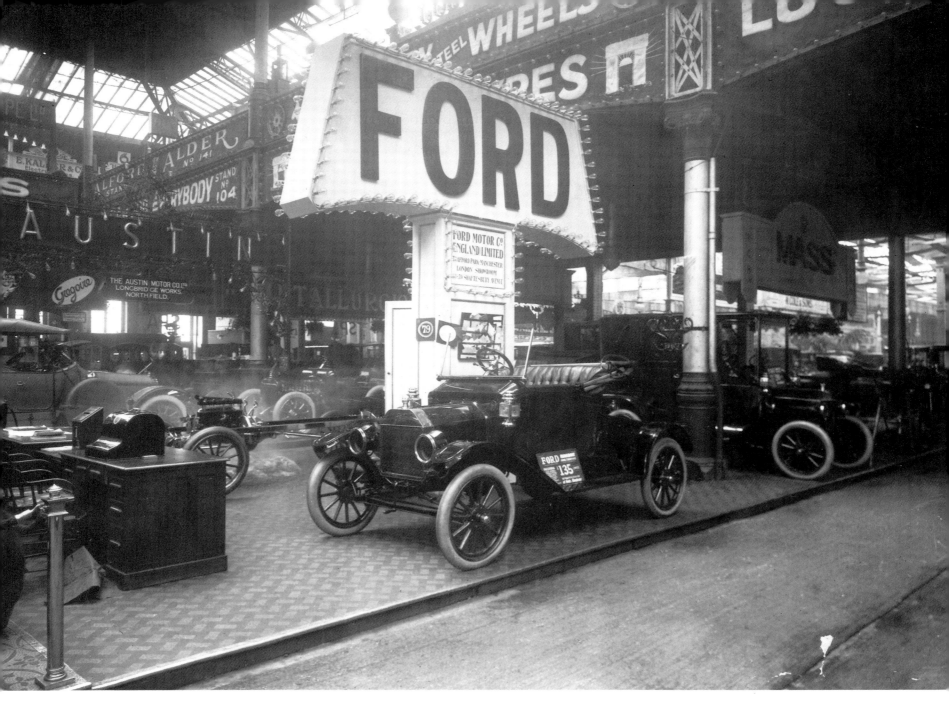

ABOVE: *Once the Model T was established in the USA, Henry Ford set up other assembly factories all over the world. One of the largest was at Trafford Park, in England. This shows the British company's Motor Show display, at Olympia in 1912, when the price was a mere £135.*

LEFT: *Model Ts eventually came in all shapes and sizes. This station wagon type was built in 1921, when the T was climbing to the peak of its popularity.*

RIGHT: *Yet another variation on a well-used theme – this was a Model T delivery van, built in 1916, and lovingly restored in the 1980s.*

In the next few years, Model T motoring grew to be so popular that the car became a part of the American dream, as familiar as Coca Cola, as ubiquitous as the air which Americans breathed, and seemingly adaptable to almost every purpose. Henry liked to call the Model T a 'universal car,' for in the beginning he thought it could go on selling for ever. Apart from body styles being gradually, but almost imperceptibly, updated, the chassis changed very little indeed; one could certainly buy spare parts for a mid-1920s Model T and fit them straight on to a 1909 model.

In its original styling, the Model T looked similar to several other spidery touring cars of the period. However, that distinctive brass radiator style soon made it stand out, as did its easily recognizable put-putting exhaust note. The chassis layout was simple in the extreme, not only because Ford wanted to make the Model T as easily repairable in Nebraska as New York, or in Delaware as in Detroit.

Front and rear suspension was by transverse leaf springs, with the axles located by radius arms, and because of the exceptional ground clearance a Model T could pick its way over – and through – the most appalling terrain. The engine itself was a simple but rugged side-valve four-cylinder design, backed by an idiosyncratic epicyclic transmission.

All in all, the Model T was an intriguing mixture of the archaic and the advanced. The transmission, for instance, might be unique and require the 'clutch' pedal to be used as a means of shifting gear, but there was no gearshift as such, and there were only two forward ratios. As with other cars, there were three foot pedals, but the right pedal operated the transmission drum brake, the center pedal engaged reverse and the left pedal operated the shift itself. The accelerator control was a stalk on the steering column, one of the strange features of Henry Fords Model T.

RIGHT: *Although the Model T's engine was a simple four-cylinder side-valve unit, it was matched to a complex epicyclic transmission. Of the three pedals, the left one operated the gear shift, the center engaged reverse, and the right the transmission brake.*

The Model T was a bumbling little car, with negligible acceleration and a top speed of under 50mph, but it was also a car that could carry on for days and days without much attention. When the time came to 'get out and get under' (a phrase from one of the popular songs written around this new phenomenon), almost every owner knew how to fix the problem, and every wayside garageman, hardware-store owner or handyman most certainly did.

It was not the Model T itself, but the changes it inspired, that did so much for Ford's reputation. It was, for instance, the first car in the world to be assembled on a moving production line; this was installed at the Highland Park, Detroit, plant – and one effect was to boost assembly from 21,000 cars in 1910 to 200,000 in 1912. This huge rise in output apparently inspired Henry Ford to announce that people 'could have any color of car they liked, as long as it was black' – it took longer, and involved more complication, to offer a choice of colors.

The '$5-dollar day' has already been mentioned, as has the need for a vast new factory – the River Rouge plant – in Detroit. The enormous boost in Ford profits was an obvious result. Henry Ford made so much money out the Model T that in 1919 he was able to buy out all the non-family shareholders at a cost of $100 million.

Even though the Model T was already beginning to look obsolescent in 1919, it was rejuvenated with the fitment of a battery and an electric starter, and carried on selling better and better than ever. No fewer than 750,000 were sold in that year alone. Ford cut prices to stimulate demand and sales rose, thus boosting profits once more. Prices were cut again, sales rose again, and profits kept on rolling in.

By 1924, selling prices started at a mere $260 – which really meant that all but the poorest could afford to go motoring if they wanted to – and nearly two million Model Ts were sold in a single season.

By this time, however, General Motors, and Chevrolet in particular, was on the up and up. The Model T's appeal gradually ebbed away and even the stubborn old Henry Ford had to admit that it should be killed off. The last Model T of all was produced in May 1927, at which time a total of 15,007,033 had been produced. It was not until the early 1970s did another phenomenon, the Volkswagen Beetle, overtake that incredible feat.

BELOW: *Although Henry Ford always meant the Model T to be a strictly utilitarian machine, some customers wanted sportier versions. This was a rather rakish coupe though built on the same chassis.*

The Mad Motorists

Peking to Paris in 1907

Then, as now, the best way to succeed in motor sport is to plan ahead. Prince Scipione Borghese thought of almost everything before tackling the Peking-Paris race in 1907. The 10,000 mile journey took 44 days of actual driving.

As it happened, there was plenty of interest, but few entries materialized. Within weeks the publicity-conscious paper had reversed the route (it was a better bet to have a finish in Paris, rather than a start), and the start was fixed for 10 June 1907.

Although more than 30 teams expressed interest in this, the first of the real automobile adventures, many withdrew as soon as they began to consider the enormity of the challenge. However, right from the start an Italian nobleman, Prince Scipione Borghese, commissioned Itala to build him a special 35/45 model and began to lay plans to do the marathon properly.

In the end only five cars mustered in Peking to make the epic journey, northwest into Mongolia and the Gobi desert, then for thousands of bleak miles across the plains of Siberia, from Tomsk to Omsk, and on to Moscow. The final leg, via Warsaw and Berlin, seemed tame by comparison. There were few roads, even fewer maps and — in every case except that of Borghese — very little forward planning by the entrants.

It was a marathon contested by some ill-prepared cars. Apart from the Itala there was Charles Godard's 15hp Spyker, Georges Cormier's 10hp De Dion, Victor Collignon's identical De Dion, and the frail, quite unsuitable, 6hp two-stroke Contal tri-car. Because of the rugged and unknown nature of the route, the five crews agreed to stay in convoy and help each other out of difficulties until they reached Irkutsk, after which the race would really get under way.

Like all such good intentions, this one fell apart at once, for two cars lost touch with the others only minutes after the

T HE world's first automobile competition was a reliability run from Paris to Rouen and back in 1895. In the next few years a series of long-distance town-to-town races turned touring into a dangerous sport for heroes. Rallying, as we now know it, did not truly develop until the 1920s. Even before the first Monte Carlo rally was held, the first of the automobile marathons had been promoted.

The headline in the leading French newspaper *Le Matin* on 31 January 1907, told its own story when translated into English, it read:

PARIS-PEKING AUTOMOBILE
A Stupendous Challenge

The paper was prepared to sponsor such an event through utterly unknown territory, but would there be any entries?

start, and by the time the Gobi Desert had been crossed Borghese's Itala was already a full day ahead. The Chinese roads were so bad that all the cars had to be dragged or man-handled up ravines, often with bodywork stripped off and provisions removed. The Contal tri-car was so underpowered and badly balanced that within a week it had dropped out.

At Urga the Borghese Itala team had forged well ahead, not least because the Prince seemed to have thought of every-thing, and had spent an enormous amount of time and money preparing for this adventure. Before the event he had arranged for supplies of fuel, tyres and provisions to be dumped at strategic points across Siberia. These had been placed by camel caravans – cars being unknown in most parts of Russia in 1907 – to await the Prince's arrival.

The cars were delayed by all manner of mishaps. At one point the Itala plunged off a rickety bridge into a ravine and had to be winched out by a gang of Siberian railway workers. The intrepid Godard resorted to intrigue, financial skulldug-gery and sharp practice to keep his underfinanced car going – it is a miracle that he did not spend a long period in jail.

Where there were no roads the cars ran alongside the Trans-Siberian railway, and at times they had to be navi-gated by compass. There were no control points, of course, and if Borghese's Itala had decided to take a 'piggy-back' trip across Siberia on a train no one would have known – the only object was to get to Paris first and claim *Le Matin*'s prize.

Prince Borghese's preparations had been so much more thorough and his car was so much faster and more rugged than his rivals', that he reached Omsk 10 days ahead of the other three cars, a gap he had stretched to 18 days by the time he arrived in Moscow. So confident was he of victory that he dallied in Moscow for a full three days, before setting out on the last 'easy' 2500 miles to Paris, which he completed in only 11 days.

Arriving in Paris on 10 August, two months after starting from Peking, Prince Borghese claimed to have driven 10,000 miles and to have spent 30,000 francs over and above his sponsorship. The three stragglers, still together, arrived in Paris 20 days later, by which time the whole affair had been forgotten.

OPPOSITE: *Only five cars started the Peking-Paris race on 10 June 1907, and this frail 6hp Contal tri-car was simply not strong enough for such a rugged trip. It dropped out within days of the 'off.'*

BELOW: *For a pioneering trip like Peking-Paris it helped to look the part and solar topees were essential items of equipment. This car was one of the De Dions which survived the journey and made it to Paris.*

For Itala it was a real triumph – especially as an Italian marque had won what *Le Matin* hoped would be a French dominated event. But fame is ephemeral. The Itala was shown at Britain's Olympia Motor Show in 1908, but later rolled into the water at Genoa docks when being shipped to New York for exhibition. After being salvaged it was stored, unrepaired, for some years, but is now on permanent exhibition at the Museo Nazionale dell'Automobile in Turin.

Bugatti Splendor

Le pur sang des automobiles

I N the first half of the twentieth century, there was a Bugatti car, and a man called Bugatti. The car most certainly could not have existed without the man.

Ettore Arco Bugatti was born in Italy in 1881, began building cars carrying his own name before World War I, and was renowned as an artist-engineer of automobiles and fascinating engines in the 1919-39 period. Although there were a few post-World War II Bugattis, these never had the same reputation, or the same pedigree, as the earlier models. Bugatti himself survived the First World War, his reputation and his factory at Molsheim (just) intact, but life had lost all meaning for him in August 1939 when his son Jean was killed in a road crash near the Alsace plant.

Until he began building his own cars at Molsheim, in what had been an abandoned dyeing works, he made his name with designs for De Dietrich, Mathis and Deutz. The Bugatti-designed De Dietrichs were all large, fast cars (especially the 1903 Paris-Madrid 50hp race car), his Mathis connection was brief, and his three years with Deutz were spent in Cologne.

The original Bugatti production car was the Type 13 of 1910-26, which later gained the title of 'Brescia' after its racing successes at a circuit near that Italian town. The last car to be built in any numbers was the famous Type 57 family of 1934-40.

The difference between these two cars was complete – the original Type 13 had a 1.3-liter four-cylinder engine and a 6-foot 7-inch wheelbase, while the fiercest of the Type 57s, the Type 57SC, had a highly tuned, supercharged, twin-overhead-camshaft 3.3-liter engine, a wheelbase of more than 9 feet and a top speed of over 100 mph. Between the two, however, was a skein of continuous design improvement that any Bugatti fanatic can trace with ease.

Along the way, Bugatti produced some really outstanding cars – none more sensational than the massive Type 41 Royale, and none more technically advanced than the four-wheel-drive Type 53 racing car of 1932. On the other hand, there were certain Bugatti features that were at once characteristic and infuriating.

For no very good technical reason, Bugatti hated the very idea of six-cylinder engines, or V-layout engines. Accordingly, every Bugatti unit ever made was either a straight four, a straight eight or (in two cases, Type 45 and Type 47 racing machines) a double eight with two eight-cylinder blocks mounted side by side on the same crankcase.

BELOW: *One of the most exclusive cars in the world. The Bugatti Type 41 Royale, of which only six were built – though none sold to royalty!*

RIGHT: *You have to look very carefully, then look again, before seeing that* this is actually a toy *Bugatti – the Type 52 of 1927.*

LOWER RIGHT: *One of the most celebrated, and classic, shapes of all time – the Type 35 GP Bugatti. Note the unique wheels, and big brakes.*

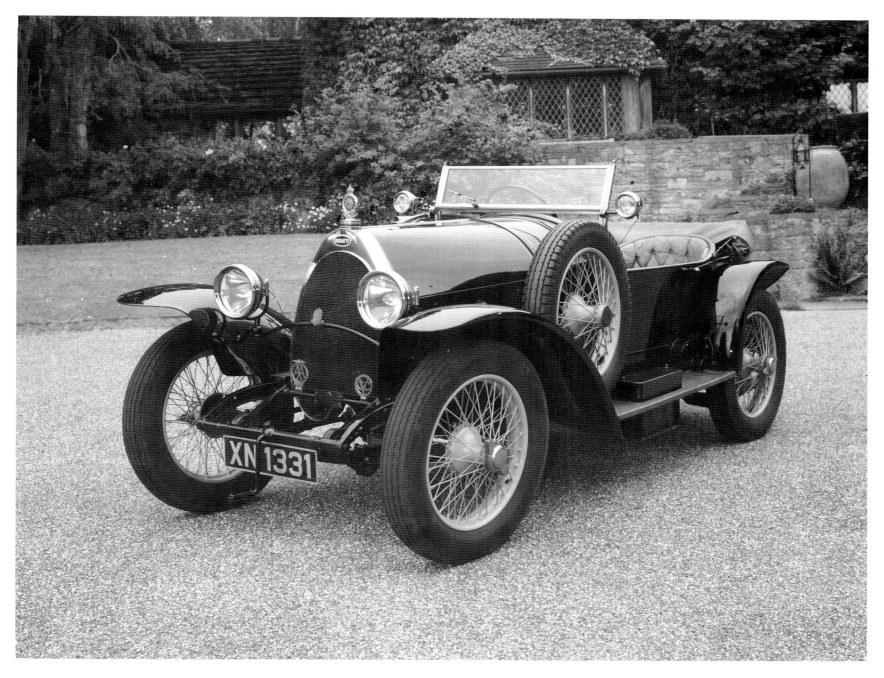

ABOVE LEFT: *Bugatti's last Grand Prix car was the Type 59.*

LEFT: *The Type 55 was an eight-cylinder 2.3-liter Super Sports car, built from 1932 to 1935.*

ABOVE: *'Black Bess' is the famous 5-liter four-cylinder Bugatti, built in 1913.*

OVERLEAF: *The 3.3-liter Type 57 was built during 1934-1939.*

OVERLEAF INSET: *The fabulous Type 57S, with Atlantic coachwork.*

Even though there was a lot of evidence to prove it desirable, Bugatti never fitted independent front suspension to his cars, nor did he ever allow synchromesh to be added to his transmissions. Throughout the life of the marque, all Bugatti models were extremely complex and difficult to repair. It used to be said that if you wanted to rebuild a Bugatti engine you started by removing the back wheels.

Until the early 1920s, Bugatti's reputation was built up on the record of the Type 13 Brescia family, but from 1924 all the previous cars were quite overshadowed by the style, the elegance and the effective performance of the Type 35 models. Here was an eight-cylinder car which helped Bugatti to dominate international racing for the rest of the 1920s, with a design that everyone now recalls with pleasure. To a simple chassis, with rock-hard leaf springs, wire-spoke or 'steel-blade' type wheels, and a sleek body headed by the characteristic Bugatti horseshoe radiator, was added that spine-tingling engine noise at speed. It was, in every way, *pur sang* (thoroughbred) – and there would be many other such Bugattis in the years to come.

In the late 1920s, however, all were overshadowed by the Type 41 Royale, which Ettore Bugatti intended to be sold to royalty. It was enormous, with a 12.7-liter overhead-camshaft engine later used in French Railways railcars, and by far the most expensive car in the world at the time. In all, only six such cars were built – none of them sold to royalty! All six survive, one was sold in 1986 for an astronomical price in excess of $8 million.

The first dual-overhead-camshaft Bugatti was the luxurious 5-liter Type 50 of 1930, after which twin-cam engines, looking just as magnificent as the single-cams had ever done, followed for the Type 51 race car (a Type 35 successor), the Type 54 race cars and all subsequent road cars from the famed Bugatti stable.

The Type 57s, for the design of which Ettore's son Jean was mainly responsible, were the most elegant and the most effective of all Molsheim-built cars. Eminent historians describe them as having 'twin-cam splendour', for they were built with a choice of wheelbases, blown or unblown engines, and a wide variety of sexy French coachbuilders' body styles. The miracle was that these cars were being built in France where politics were moving steadily to the left, and at a time when almost every feature except the engine was obsolete. A triumph of style over function.

The Bugatti ethic can never be explained to anyone who has neither seen nor driven one of these fine cars. The task is like describing an elephant to a blind man – impossible unless he can experience it for himself. In its way, and in its day, the Bugatti had no direct rivals. There has been nothing like it since.

Mercedes-Benz

Setting a standard for others to follow

IN spite of fierce competition, the humiliating aftermath of World War I, and the economic blizzard that engulfed Germany in the early 1920s, two proud car-making companies – Daimler and Benz – held on to their stability and actually increased their standing in the world of the automobile. However, few companies had enough resources, or enough guaranteed sales, to make it through hyper-inflation without help, and in the end the two German giants had to get together to survive. In 1924 Daimler and Benz agreed to cooperate in some respects, and in 1926 a formal merger was arranged.

Thereafter, the company became known as Daimler-Benz and the products were always marketed as Mercedes-Benz.

The plain three-pointed (Daimler) star atop the radiators was replaced by a three-pointed star surrounded by a laurel wreath and labelled 'Mercedes-Benz.'

For some years, cars continued to be made in two locations, at the Daimler factories in Stuttgart and at the old Benz plant in Mannheim. It was not until the 1930s that all car assembly was concentrated on Stuttgart, and it was not until after World War II that chassis and final assembly lines were moved to the previous body-construction factory at Sindelfingen on the outskirts of the city.

Daimler-Benz's most obvious assets were its design engineers, for the new board of management included three truly famous personalities – Dr Ferdinand Porsche and Fritz Nallinger from Daimler, and Hans Nibel from Benz. It was no wonder that there were both outstanding new products and enormous boardroom battles to come, in the next few years.

The most exciting late-1920s Mercedes-Benz cars were the supercharged six-cylinder models that Porsche had started to evolve when he joined Daimler a few years earlier. These all featured supercharging that could be 'clutched' into operation by an emphatic movement of the throttle foot, a process which was usually accompanied by the scream of the hard-working engine.

This design started life with a 100hp engine (140hp with supercharger engaged), which explains its original title of 24/100/140, but within a few years the engine had been

BELOW: *In 1901 Daimler introduced the new, low-slung Mercedes range. This is a 120hp derivative of 1905.*

OPPOSITE: *Mercedes used motor sport to develop, and*

to publicize its models, here a 1922 Targa Florio.

OPPOSITE BELOW: *Edwardian Mercedes cars, like this example, had flat radiators, and three-pointed star badges.*

U2757(

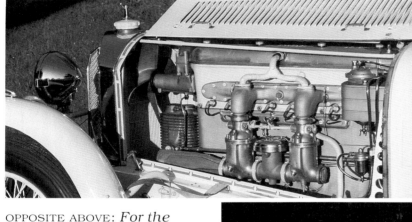

OPPOSITE ABOVE: *For the 1914 French GP, Mercedes built a fleet of new 4½-liter cars, which won the race.*

OPPOSITE: *The most famous pre-1914 Benz is the massive 200hp 'Blitzen' model, which had a 21.5-liter engine.*

TOP: *The most famous of Dr Porsche's supercharged 'sixes' built for Mercedes – the SSK model.*

ABOVE: *Seven liters of supercharged 38/250 'SS' engine.*

RIGHT: *The Mercedes-Benz SS, or 38/250 model, had a blown 7-liter six-cylinder engine.*

enlarged to no less than 7 liters and boosted still further. The chassis design was shortened, lowered and made lighter, with the result that the exclusive SSK sports car had ratings of 170/225hp and a top speed of more than 100mph, while the ultra-light SSKL (L for *Leicht*) could dispose of up to 300hp in race-car trim.

Porsche, meanwhile, had left Daimler-Benz after a blazing row with his fellow directors, so it was Hans Nibel who was responsible for the next Mercedes-Benz 'Supercar.' If the previous cars had already set standards for others to follow, this one took the marque even farther ahead.

The flagship, launched in 1930, was the Type 770 Grosser-model, a monster intended for use by politicians, potentates and tycoons. It was an enormous car, with typically flamboyant coachwork, and was powered by a straight eight-cylinder engine of 7.7 liters with the well-proven type of 'optional' supercharging. Customers included ex-Kaiser Wilhelm II of Germany and Emperor Hirohito of Japan.

Its successor, produced only in 1938 and 1939 for Nazi party bosses and their lackeys to use, was another 770 Grosser, still with the same engine (and up to 230hp when supercharged), but with a new tubular chassis frame, independent front suspension and De Dion rear suspension (all inspired by Grand Prix Mercedes-Benz models of the day). Not only did it look impressive, but it weighed up to 8000 pounds (with *no* power steering), could reach 110 mph, and rarely recorded more than 5 miles per gallon. Only 88 such cars were built.

Daimler-Benz also produced a series of flamboyant super-charged six-cylinder cars (the 500K and 540K Series) during

the 1930s, which were really softened-down, rather 'trans-atlantic' successors to the SSK models. But the company's most significant contribution to automobile engineering in the 1930s was in the realm of quantity-production cars.

In 1931 the new Type 170 was revealed, not only with a box section chassis at a time when most rivals were still using channel frames, but with independent front *and* rear suspension. A few years later the development of this advanced chassis was mated to the world's first passenger-car diesel engine, a 2.6-liter unit which naturally led to it being called the Type 260D.

Not only that, but in the mid-1930s Hans Nibel's design team finally came round to Porsche's thinking and produced a rear-engined car for sale. This was the Type 130H (H for *Heck*, or 'Rear'), which had a 1.3-liter engine and only 26hp,

but still had rather unmanageable handling characteristics; later the larger-engined 170H was also produced. The limited-production 150H was in fact a mid-engined 55hp overhead-cam 1.5-liter sports derivative of this layout, but very few were made. By comparison, the front-engined 170V of the late 1930s was an enormous success, with more than 90,000 vehicles being built before car production was stopped in 1942.

All this helped boost Mercedes-Benz output to unheard-of heights. About 28,000 cars a year were being assembled by 1938. At the same time the company was also dominating the truck markets, and with its excellent V12 aero-engines was preparing to supply power to the Luftwaffe's fighters and bombers. By any reckoning the between-wars Daimler-Benz concern was a standard-setter for the rest of Europe.

LEFT: *In 1930, Mercedes-Benz launched the Type 770 Grosser-model, with supercharged 7.6-liter engine, producing up to 200hp. There was a six-speed gearbox, and some cars weighed nearly 6000lb. Only 117 cars of this type were built; this particular chauffeur-driven example was supplied to ex-Kaiser Wilhelm II.*

98082

ABOVE: *Four generations of successful British land speed records. From the bottom: 350hp Sunbeam; twin-engined '1000hp' Sunbeam of 1927; Golden Arrow of 1929: the 1964 gas-turbined Bluebird.*

BELOW: *Malcolm (later Sir Malcolm) Campbell sits inside the 350hp Sunbeam Land Speed Record car of 1924.*

The Vintage Car

A European phenomenon

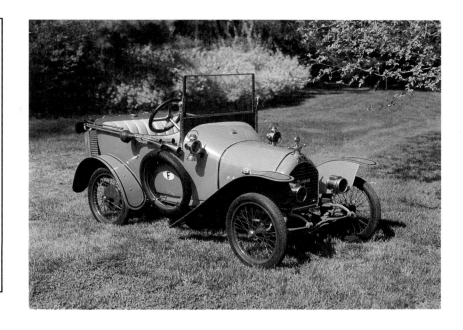

T HE phrase 'vintage car' was not invented until 1934, when a new British automobile club was founded. The enthusiasts who joined to set up this organization were all bound together by the same beliefs – that the best cars in the world had been produced between the close of World War I and the end of 1930, and that no worthwhile cars had been produced since then.

ABOVE: *A typical European car of the early 1920s, the French-manufactured Peugeot 'Bébé.'*

BELOW: *Citroën's first cars were sold in 1919, and for years were simple, solid, no-nonsense vintage machines. This was a 5CV of 1923.*

Having decided to worship only one age of the automobile (and who is to say whether such enthusiasts were misguided?), the cars had to be defined and the club given a name. Since it was thought that these cars were the best, the vocabulary of fine wines was 'borrowed.' The cars became 'vintage' and the club the Vintage Sports Car Club (VSCC).

To anyone living outside Europe, and especially to any enthusiast in North America, the phrase 'vintage car' has very little meaning. Americans have their own ideas of what constitutes a fine car, and to them such a car is a 'classic' if it was built between 1925 and 1948, dates that in turn mean very little to Europeans.

Officially, therefore, a vintage car is one built between 1919 and the end of 1930, though this rigid definition brings all kinds of anomalies in its wake. Presumably we must assume that a Rolls-Royce Phantom II built in 1929 or 1930 is vintage, but that one built in 1934 or 1935 is not? Strange — especially as the later models in any series tend to be better built than the originals.

It is worth mentioning, however, another VSCC category, the 'post-vintage thoroughbred', which allows fine cars of the 1930s to have some semblance of respectability. Sports cars like the Meadows-engined Lagondas, some Frazer Nashes and some Aston Martins qualify.

Everyone has their own idea of what a typical vintage car looks like, goes like and, above all, feels like. Vintage motoring is not merely measured by 0-60mph figures, by sizes, weights and shapes, but by character. The vintage movement favors those cars that were built by craftsmen, often in relatively small workshops, and in limited numbers. But the definition of 'vintage' is so all-embracing that it covers a hand-built Bentley and a mass-produced Austin Seven, a Type 35 Bugatti racing car and a workaday Morris 'bullnose' model. The sheer variety of fine cars built in this period is astonishing — and all count as vintage.

Let us look at the anatomy of a typical vintage car — the 'bullnose' Morris of the early and mid-1920s. This typifies what a vintage car, and vintage motoring, is all about.

The basis of a 'bullnose' was a rather whippy, separate chassis, mounted above the line of the axles throughout, with a forged-section front axle and a welded 'banjo' rear axle. Front and rear suspension was by half-elliptic leaf springs, and damping was by adjustable Hartford friction shock absorbers.

A 'bullnose' was steered by worm and wheel, with a long straight steering column leading back into the driving compartment. Wheels were detachable steel 'artillery-style', fitted with narrow 'balloon' tires. By the mid-1920s there were front and rear drum brakes, operated by a foot pedal or a hand lever, all being intricately connected, balanced and counterbalanced by rods, levers and cross-shafts.

The side-valve four-cylinder engine was mounted well back in the frame, there was a simple single-plate clutch, and a four-speed transmission, with a long gearshift growing straight up out of the top cover.

The 'bullnose,' like most vintage cars, was sold with a choice of body styles. All used the same front end and characteristic radiator, but there were many variations aft of the windshield. All were simply built of metal or fabric panels affixed to a wooden body-skeleton, with minimal protection against corrosion. They had front and rear fenders connected by stout running boards. The headlamps were freestanding, between the radiator and the fenders. The spare wheel was usually clamped to the tail, but sometimes tucked into a well on one of the running boards.

Windshields, without exception, were lofty and vertical, often with opening sections to allow better visibility on rainy days. Whether the cars were two-seater or four-seater tourers, four/five-seater sedans, or some variation on the theme, there was usually a generous amount of leg room, but rather

TOP: *Not only a well-known vintage car, but a vintage sports car — the Alvis 12/50 was a smart and lively 1½-liter four-cylinder British car.*

ABOVE: *Vincenzo Lancia founded his Italian firm in 1906, and built many fine vintage sports cars. This is a 1929 'Torpedo' bodied Lambda.*

OPPOSITE ABOVE: *Love them or hate them — it doesn't matter — the Ford Motor Company's Model T was the typical American vintage car of the 1920s.*

OPPOSITE: *Some of the finest vintage sports cars were of French manufacture. This was a 1930 example of the Delage D8, with bodywork by Chapron.*

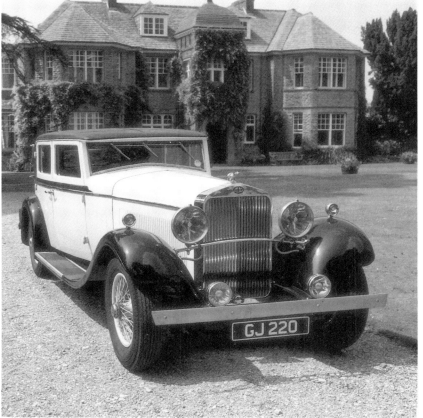

restricted width. The rear seats were usually on top of the line of the back axle, making a high roof line essential. (As car styles changed in the next 20 years or so, the width inside a body gradually increased, while the amount of sprawling room, especially in the rear seats, was gradually reduced.)

A sports car with a small engine – such as an Aston Martin or a Bugatti – was altogether lower, narrower, and very rarely sold with any other than a two-seater style, while large-engined sports cars like the archetypal vintage Bentleys were as lofty as any sedan, very bulky and very heavy.

All, however, had the same sort of 'feel' about them. The shift mechanism was positive, if not light, the steering was direct, if not necessarily easy, the engines solidly reliable. Bodies were practical, solid and quite devoid of 'flash.' Equipment was complete where fittings were essential and there was nothing to make the ensemble vulgar. There was, indeed, a rightness about a good vintage car – a rightness that was soon to be lost.

What happened in the 1930s? With the advent of a new ability to press compound curves into large pieces of sheet-metal came the one-piece steel turret-top, full-width styling and, eventually, unitary construction. In brief, cost-saving took precedence over quality, gimmicks over practicality and mass-production over craftsmanship. Perhaps the founder members of the VSCC had something, after all?

Motoring Tycoons and their Cars

Royce, Sloan, Morris and Ford

L OOK around the automobile industry today and it's run by corporate boards; the buccaneering pioneers like Durant and Cord are gone; the engineers-turned-entrepreneur like Henry Ford and Walter Chrysler have passed as well.

Yet the birth of almost every one of the world's outstanding marques was inspired by one man, who went on to dominate his firm for a good many years. Consider famous car names like Rolls-Royce, Ford, Opel, Honda and Chrysler – these all stemmed from the personalities behind them. It is a sad fact, though, that when the founder died or retired, there was rarely another member of his family ready to take over.

The largest companies of all – General Motors, Nissan, Volkswagen and Fiat – were not named after a founder, but in their formative years they all had one strong man at the top. But you are excused if you do not recall these men – that was the way it was always intended. Until the 1920s, however, there seemed to be automobile tycoons all around, and some became as famous as the cars they were building.

TOP: *Henry Royce (with beard) was Rolls-Royce's technical chief for nearly 30 years. Ernest Hives, to his left, later became the company's chairman.*

ABOVE: *Alfred P Sloan brought order to General Motors in the 1920s, and inspired the birth of this successful type of Chevrolet.*

There is no doubt who was the most famous of all – that was Henry Ford. In spite of his apparent 'hillbilly' manners and simplistic attitudes, he never shunned the limelight. Not only was he the chief designer – the only designer, really – of the legendary Model T, but for many years he and his close family were the only shareholders in the company.

As his many biographers have discovered, Henry Ford's personality was a puzzling paradox. On the one hand there was the businessman wise enough to invest in the automobile industry's first moving assembly line and to use the successful 'bring down prices and we'll sell more cars' gambit, but on the other hand there was the naive pacifist who financed the notorious 'peace ship' initiative to Europe during World War I, in the hope that he could stop the fighting merely with a gesture.

It was Ford, too, who once referred to history as being 'mostly bunk,' yet set up the Greenfield Village and the Henry Ford Museum, in Detroit, to preserve it. And it was Ford who refused to have union recognition in his plants. He was brilliant enough to see that the Model T was exactly what the American public needed, but blind enough not to see that it was obsolete by 1927. His thinking never moved with the times, and if it had not been for the rush of contracts gained to build military machinery during World War II, the company might not have survived the 1940s.

His son, Edsel, died young, and it was his grandson, Henry Ford II, who put the company back on an even keel once again in the post-war years.

Ford's real rival in Detroit in the 1920s was Alfred P. Sloan, the guiding genius behind the steady rise of General Motors. The company had been founded in 1908, but was a muddled mess of several competing businesses when Sloan became executive vice-president in 1921. In the next decade he shook out the whole group, systematized it, saw it buy overseas subsidiaries and take over market leadership from Ford. Before long GM was the world's largest industrial company. In every way, it was Sloan's lasting epitaph, for after he had gone from the chief executive's chair in 1946, General Motors came to be ruled by a succession of faceless men — few of whom will be remembered outside of the industry.

ABOVE: *Henry Ford controlled every aspect of his own company until the mid-1940s, although not always with wisdom or foresight.*

BELOW: *To replace the obsolete Model T, Ford rushed through the all-new, conventional Model A in 1927. This is a 1929 version.*

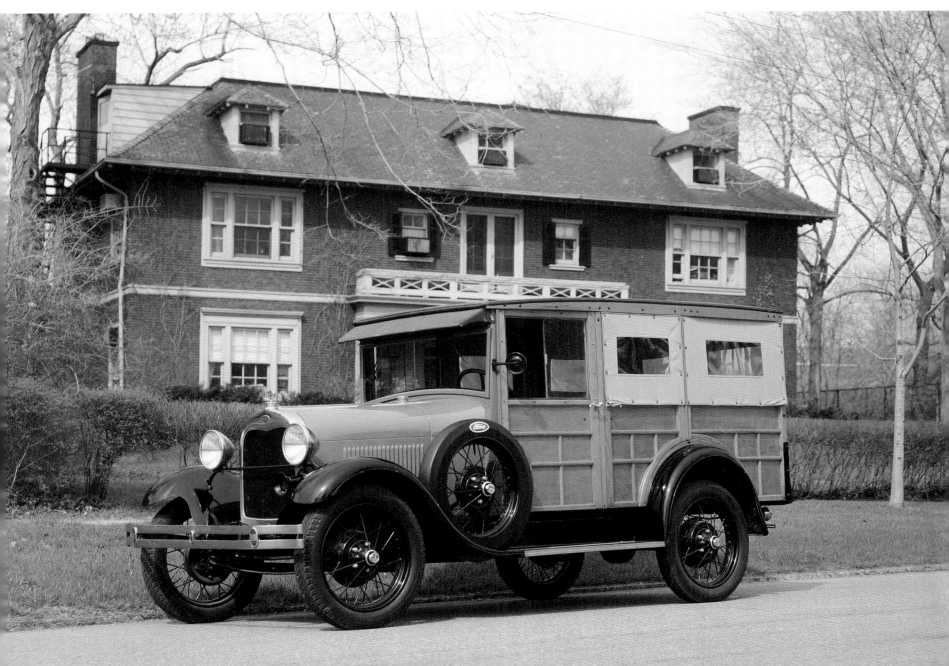

In Britain, three motoring tycoons dominated the period between the two World Wars, each in his own way – Henry Royce, Herbert Austin and William Morris. By 1939, Sir Henry Royce had died, while the other two had been elevated to the peerage.

Royce was an electrical engineer by training, but always liked to describe himself merely as a 'mechanic.' His links with the Hon. Charles Rolls (a member of the gentry, noted salesman and sportsman) led to the birth of the Rolls-Royce car, but after Rolls was killed in an airplane crash in 1910 Royce was on his own. Even before World War I Royce had suffered a major operation, becoming a semi-invalid. He therefore handed over the general day-to-day management of his company to others and spent the next 20 years designing everything from a complete aero-engine to the details of a chassis.

In Royce's view there was only one way to design a car – the best way – which explains why it took so long to develop a new Rolls-Royce, why the price was high, and why the marque was, and is, so revered. Nevertheless, the West owes more to Royce as the inspiration behind the Merlin V12 engine, which powered thousands of Spitfire, Lancaster and Mosquito aircraft during World War II. He died in 1933.

William Morris, who became Lord Nuffield in the 1930s, started life as a pedal-cycle repairer and graduated to Morris car production in 1913. His method, well-proven in practice, was to start by buying in as much of his cars as possible, and then take over the company that was doing a particular job best of all. Morris Motors, therefore, became big by acquisition, and rarely spent more on capital investment or original design than was absolutely necessary.

Lord Nuffield, who had no children, personally ruled Morris (and eventually MG, Wolseley and Riley) from 1913 to 1952, when it became a part the British Motor Corporation

(BMC), after which he retired from business life. Along the way he had given away tens of millions of pounds, for medical and other good causes. He died in 1963.

Herbert Austin (Lord Austin in his final years) started working with Wolseley in the 1880s, designed the first Wolseley car in 1896, and set up the Austin Motor Co. in 1905. From small beginnings at Longbridge, south of Birmingham, his company grew rapidly, until in the 1920s and 1930s it shared market leadership with Morris Motors. Unlike Morris, Herbert Austin was a gifted engineer and designer, among whose triumphs was the design of the Austin Seven baby car. He also believed in making as much as possible of his cars 'in-house' and had turned Longbridge into a proper manufacturing complex by the late 1930s.

When the time came for him to retire, he recruited Leonard Lord to run the business. Austin died in 1941, but Leonard Lord expanded Austin considerably after that, masterminded the Austin-Nuffield merger in 1952, and became the undisputed 'king of BMC' (British Motor Corporation) in the 1950s and 1960s.

61

America's Great Depression

Boom to bust, then boom again

COMPARED with France and Germany, the United States automobile industry was late on the scene, but it made up for this with huge expansion in the 1910s and 1920s. Then came the Wall Street Crash of October 1929, which changed everything.

Once the American stock market collapsed, so did the American economy and business confidence in general. In 1927 the North American automobile industry had produced three million cars, and in 1928 this roared ahead to four million. The peak figure, in 1929, was four and a half million; four out of five cars built anywhere in the world were being produced in North America. Then came the Crash, sales plummeted, stocks of unsold cars rose rapidly and many garage businesses plunged into bankruptcy. The 1929 record would not be beaten for another 20 years.

For automobile enthusiasts who were unaffected by such financial traumas, there was the sight of gloriously engineered new cars arriving on the American scene just as

BELOW: *The magnificent eight-cylinder Duesenberg Model J arrived at exactly the wrong moment in America's industrial history . . .*

INSET: *Everything about the L-29 Cord was superlative – eight-cylinder engine, front-wheel-drive and a $3000 price – but it was badly timed for the Wall Street Crash of 1929.*

their potential buyers lost all their money, jumped ship, or stepped out of skyscraper windows to end it all on the sidewalks below.

After all, if it had not been for their confidence in America's future, Cadillac would certainly not have produced a 7.4-liter V16 engined model in 1930, Cord would not have produced the straight-eight front-wheel-drive L29, nor Ruxton an eight-cylinder 5.5-liter model, nor Duesenberg the fabulously detailed Model J, which had a 6.9-liter eight-cylinder engine, dual overhead camshafts, four valves per cylinder and 200hp.

However, it was not only the large, expensive marques that suffered. Those customers who might have bought Chevrolets, Fords and Buicks were also hard hit, and all car makers suffered badly. Just look at these figures:

Ford sold 1.1 million cars in 1930, 615,000 in 1931, but only 211,000 in 1932.

Chevrolet sold 641,000 cars in 1930, 620,000 in 1931 but only 313,000 in 1932.

Buick sold 182,000 cars in 1930, 139,000 in 1931, but only 57,000 in 1932.

This experience was shared right across the product range. Between 1929 and 1932, total car production plummeted by 75 percent.

The miracle was that the industry's tycoons did not lose their nerve. Most were forced to lay off tens of thousands of their workers and close down assembly lines, but they had made enough money to hang on during the Depression.

It also gave the opportunity for companies to rationalize and to bring in advanced features. General Motors had

ABOVE: *Cars like the Ford V8 of the mid and late 1930s helped pull the big companies out of the Depression years.*

RIGHT: *Maybe it was technically advanced, but most people also thought it ugly – Chrysler's Airflow of the mid 1930s.*

OPPOSITE: *When the Depression had eased, Cord made another attempt to sell front-wheel-drive cars. This was the Buehrig-designed Type 812 of 1936.*

already introduced synchromesh in 1928, but it was the 1930s which saw the arrival in large quantities of independent front suspension, overdrive and fully-automatic transmission, rubber engine mounts, hydraulic brakes, all-steel bodies, and more streamlined and rounded styling. Chrysler dabbled with streamlined styling (on the Airflow, which was a miserable failure), while Ford produced the world's first mass-production V8 power unit.

Even though President Franklin D Roosevelt's 'New Deal' of 1933 helped to get the United States gradually back on its feet economically and to regain its self-confidence once

more, it took time for the car companies to recover. Indeed, some never made it.

By 1940, only a few independent manufacturers were left. Famous American names that disappeared in this troubled decade included Essex, Hupmobile, Pierce-Arrow, Marmon and the combination of Auburn, Cord and Duesenberg. Other companies were forced to trim their sails to stay alive: Lincoln, for instance, turned from making individual high-price cars to building large quantities based on Ford engineering. Even Rolls-Royce was forced to close down its Springfield, Massachusetts, factory in 1931.

The big names fought their way through, though the pecking order changed somewhat. Ford, having lost the sales lead to Chevrolet during the Depression, was well on top during the late 1930s (mainly because of the new V8 engine and remarkably low prices).

The Ford group, however, lost ground to the Chrysler Corporation, which had been newly founded in the 1920s, and which overtook it. Ford's problem was that it was still ruled by the quixotic founder and lacked a proper range of cars. Chrysler also had Plymouth, Dodge and De Soto to sell — which they did, in profusion.

As the traditional names faded away, America's 'top people' were reduced to a choice of just three fine cars —

Lincoln, Packard and Cadillac. And once the lovely old Model K Lincoln died and Packard moved down market, the Cadillac was left on its own.

One way to sum up Detroit's problems in the 1930s is by noting that there were 31 separate marques in 1930, but only 17 by 1942 (when private car production closed down on the outbreak of war). Another way, though, is to recall that the nation pulled steadily out of the Depression and was building 3.7 million cars a year again by 1936. Boom to bust to boom again in only seven years? Only the American automobile business could have achieved such a feat of industrial reorganisation in such a short time, and with so much obvious success.

RIGHT: *Edsel Ford saw a market niche for an up-market version of the Lincoln. This was the original 4.8-liter Continental (later known as 'Mk 1') built until 1948.*

BELOW: *During the 1930s, Ford phased out the exclusive Lincolns, in favor of the Ford-derived Lincoln Zephyrs, which had side-valve V12 engines. This Model 902 was built in 1936.*

Great British Sports Cars

For the young-at-heart, everywhere

ABOVE: *To many people, the typical British sports car of the 1930s was the MG* *Midget. This is actually the first of the 'Nuffield' Midgets of 1936.*

ALTHOUGH Britain certainly did not invent the sports car, it was the first country to build such machines at low prices and in large numbers. Not only MG in the 1930s, but Austin-Healey, Jaguar, MG and Triumph in the 1950s and 1960s did much to bring wind-in-the-hair driving to enthusiasts all over the world.

Cecil Kimber, and Morris Garages in Oxford, started it all in the 1920s, with their special-bodied Morris models which they christened MG. But it was the Midgets and Magnettes that followed which really popularized sports cars in Britain.

Like many of the cars that followed, these MGs were small, nimble, with rakish styling and an enormous amount of exuberant character. To keep down the costs, much of the running gear was modified from mass-production units.

The M-Type, J2, PA and PB two-seaters were eventually replaced by the MG T-Series models, which ran from 1936 to 1955. It was the TC, of 1945-50, which introduced British sports cars to the United States market, while the TD that followed was the first Midget to have independent front suspension. Even though the cars' styling changed a little over the years, all of them carried the same traditional looks with woodframed bodies, flowing fenders and easily recognizable radiators. Heaters, wind-up windows and wind-cheating styles were not provided.

To rival MG, Singer produced the Le Mans models, and Triumph produced some nice Southern Cross models, but few could match the prices. Marques such as Frazer Nash, Aston Martin and Lagonda were much more expensive.

The real boom in Great British Sports Cars came after World War II. Economic conditions made it necessary for most cars to be exported and the United States market was huge and potentially profitable, so several companies designed sports cars to appeal to that vast continent. They were, of course, sold in competition with US-built sports cars such as Mercer and Stutz.

MG, having led the way for so long, was still making the 1930s-style TD in 1952 when two new cars threatened to sweep the company away. One was the Austin-Healey 100, the other the Triumph TR2. It was not until MG's beautiful new MGA arrived in 1955 that the Abingdon-based company was back on terms. In the next two decades these cars, and their descendants, fought for every sale.

Triumph's TR2 became TR3, then TR3A, all with the same style, before the Michelotti-styled TR4 took over in 1961. This was succeeded by the TR4A in 1965, which in turn gave way

to the six-cylinder TR5/TR250 cars in 1967. With a restyle by Karmann, to become the TR6, this line carried on to 1976 – a phenomenal record. At the peak of demand, more than 20,000 TRs were being built every year, most going to the United States.

It was the same story from Austin-Healey, for the four-cylinder engined 100 became the six-cylinder 100 Six, and then the 3000, before the last car was built in 1968. The Austin-Healey was a much prettier machine that the TR, and

exactly the sort of car you need to pose along the boulevards and promenades of the world.

MG's MGA was also a pretty car, especially in bubble-top coupe guise. It progressed from 1500cc in 1955, to 1600cc in 1959, and 1600 MK II in 1961, before giving way to the completely redesigned MGB of 1962. MGAs had separate chassis frames, but the MGB was a rigid monocoque model; it went on to sell even better than the MGA had done, with more than 500,000 delivered in the next 18 years.

OPPOSITE: *The hand-built British sports car at its best. The post-war Frazer Nash had a tubular frame and a Bristol engine.*

OPPOSITE BELOW: *Now more valuable than it was when current, this is the 'bug-eye' Austin-Healey Sprite of 1958-61.*

RIGHT: *More than 100,000 MG MGAs were built between 1955 and 1962, most being sold in the USA.*

BELOW: *David Brown's revived Aston Martin company built the DB2 family from 1950 to 1959. This is a 1953 DB2/4.*

OPPOSITE: *The classic Triumph TR of 1953-1962. This is the 2-liter TR3A with wide-mouth grille.*

OPPOSITE BELOW: *The first practical Lotus road car was the backbone-framed Elan, introduced in 1962.*

ABOVE: *Between 1962 and 1980, more than 500,000 MG MGBs were built. The 'black bumper' style was introduced for 1975.*

BELOW: *The Lotus Elan Plus 2 had 2+2 seating, but the same good Lotus handling.*

Then there were the Jaguar XK sports cars, which used that magnificent dual-overhead-camshaft engine and looked so stunning; the Morgans, stuck in a styling timewarp they have never shaken off; and the Jowett Jupiter, so nearly a very successful two-seater.

The real breakthrough, however, came as the 1950s ended, when both BMC and Triumph repeated their success, this time at an altogether smaller and cheaper level. The Austin-Healey Sprite of 1958, instantly nicknamed 'bug-eye' because of its bulgy-headlamp styling, took sports car motoring back to MG Midget dimensions. Restyled in 1961, it also took on a near-identical running mate which *was* called an MG Midget. Soon after this Triumph produced the pretty little Spitfire as a head-on rival. Because prices were even lower (one could buy an early Midget for less than $1800, a real bargain), the Americans loved these cars even more than their larger cousins and they kept the cash registers ringing for years. Midgets were made until 1979 and Spitfires until 1980, with 356,000 and 314,000 respectively being built.

Then, of course, there were all the derivatives, such as the six-cylinder Triumph GT6 Coupes, the six-cylinder MG MGCs and the V8 engined MGB GT V8 Coupes of the 1970s. It was a time for the British manufacturers to be proud, for although Fiat and Alfa Romeo both tried hard, with pretty cars and exciting specifications, they could not match the British value-for-money.

Nevertheless, the steam had gone out of the market for British manufacturers by the 1970s, and Triumph's wedge-styled TR7 was not nearly as well received as the mid-engined Fiat X1/9. Datsun's Z-Car coupes also came along to take over where the Austin-Healey had left off. By the 1980s sales of open two-seater sports cars had slumped. An era had ended.

Hitler's Dream Car

The VW Beetle project

ABOVE: *The VW Beetle was conceived to realize Adolf Hitler's 'people's car' project. Here, Hitler takes part in celebrations to mark the foundation of the Wolfsburg factory.*

OPPOSITE ABOVE: *The 1939 streamlined Beetle, produced for the projected Berlin-Rome-Berlin race.*

OPPOSITE: *The early Beetles had no rear window.*

A S far as car drivers are concerned, the only good thing to come out of Adolf Hitler's 'Thousand Year Reich' of 1933-45 was his *Volkswagen* (People's Car) project; it had other names, too, but everyone now remembers it as the amazing Volkswagen (VW) Beetle. More than 20 million Beetles of all types have been made, a world record by a very considerable margin.

The German dictator, however, did not live to see his dream car go into production. It was conceived and developed in the 1930s, but was not put on sale before the end of World War II.

This story really begins with Dr Ferdinand Porsche and a series of small-car prototypes his design bureau produced for German companies like Zündapp and NSU in the early 1930s. Hitler came to power in 1933 and declared a pet project to motorize the masses. By 1934 Porsche's dreams for a cheap-to-build, ultra-reliable people's car were known to Hitler, who signed him up, setting the impossible target of designing a car to sell for less than 1000 Reichmarks, which was the equivalent of only £90. Even in the 1930s, that was a very small sum of money to pay for a car, and Porsche always thought it ridiculous.

The chosen design looked ahead to the time when drivers could cruise for hours at any speed they wanted (especially as part of Hitler's master plan was to build thousands of miles of dual-carriageway roads). Porsche, therefore, arranged for the KdF – *Kraft durch Freude Wagen* (Strength through Joy Car) – to have a sturdy chassis, all-independent suspension and an air-cooled flat four-cylinder engine mounted in the tail. The body shape was practical, rather than stylish. Although it was not attractive, it was certainly a good windcheater. Purely because of its humpbacked shape, the car gained the nickname 'Beetle,' a sobriquet which has been directly translated into many languages over the years.

Hitler wanted everything about this state-owned car project to be special, so he sent out his experts to acquire land, to build a factory, and then to build a town close by to house the workforce. The massive industrial complex at Wolfsburg near Hamburg, which came into existence according to this Nazi vision, and which is now building the modern generation of VW cars, covers land that was open countryside before construction began in 1938.

The new car was ready to be shown by that time, but not ready to go on sale, and when war broke out in 1939 production plans were put back again and again. Until 1945 the new Wolfsburg plant mainly built military versions of the VW Beetle (including one amphibious model called the *schwimmwagen*), and it received a great deal of attention from Allied bombers.

Production of Beetle passenger cars got under way in 1945, under British Army control, and built up slowly in the next few years: 1785 were built in 1945, 10,020 in 1946, 19,244 in 1948, and no fewer than 90,038 in 1950. The Beetle phenomenon was under way. There was to be no stopping the rising demand and production rate of this car until the 1960s when popularity reached its peak.

The miracle was that such a car could sell in such large numbers. It certainly did not sell on its styling or its performance, but on its reliability, its unburstable engine, and on the way it resisted corrosion and general decay. Yet many people agree that it looked ugly, that it had a cramped interior, and that it had very dodgy roadholding when pushed hard around corners.

VW's management team, led by Heinz Nordhoff, not only pushed up the production rate, but also kept on introducing modifications – changes to make the car even more reliable, even more longlived, but rarely to make it any quicker. Most Beetle customers bought their cars because the engine could not freeze up in icy weather, and because they had more traction on slippery conditions than all their rivals. The car's body was so well sealed that many owners found it impossible to slam a door unless one of the windows was cracked open, and its ability to float was demonstrated – voluntarily or accidentally – on many occasions.

By 1952 the original type of post-war 'split-window' Beetle was selling well, and exports to the USA were growing fast.

INSET: *The Beetle's great strength was that it could handle most road conditions with great reliability; it was exported throughout the world. This is a British model.*

ABOVE: *One of many Beetle derivatives was the smart Karmann-Ghia coupe. which was introduced in 1955.*

BELOW: *The Beetle chassis and the air-cooled engine were so rugged that the 'Dune Buggy' was invented in the USA to test the Beetle to the utmost.*

In the first few years, deliveries were confined to Europe, but by the late 1950s export traffic was going all over the world. By this time half of all VW's Beetle production went to the United States, where the car built up a faithful cult following. As with the Model T Ford of the 1920s, in the 1960s the car you were most likely to find in a New York street, a jungle village of South America or the snows of Scandinavia was a VW Beetle.

The Beetle also went into production in other countries, notably in Mexico and Brazil. It is still made in Mexico to this day. Over the years the specification improved steadily, though the styling changed little. The air-cooled 1.1-liter engine became a 1.2, a 1.3, a 1.5 and finally a 1.6-liter, the transmission got synchromesh and eventually a semi-automatic option, the front suspension was changed, the rear suspension was changed, the trunk was enlarged, and Convertible and Karmann-Ghia coupe versions were put on sale – but the basic Beetle concept stayed the same.

A squared-up style, called the Type 3 1500, was announced in 1961, but did not appeal as much as the original, though the Type 2 Transporter van derivative soon became a bestseller. Beetle sales finally passed the Model T's record in February 1972, and it was only after the new front-engined/front-drive Golf was launched in 1974 that sales dropped away.

One day, no doubt, the Beetle will die off, by which time its production total will be out of reach of every other car in the world. The Beetle is unique, in every way.

What's Good for America is Good for General Motors

USA's mass car-maker

Already General Motors had its own body-building subsidiary (Fisher Body), a company producing refrigeration (Frigidaire), a finance company, and many other offshoots. When Alfred P Sloan became General Motors' executive vice-president in the 1920s, he described it as an overcomplicated business. For the next two generations Sloan and his successors struggled with a colossus that kept on growing, striving to make it as profitable and manageable as possible. This is because Sloan invented marketing and planned obsolescence (the annual styling change) and opened the first auto-styling house in the world – employing Harley Earl, the most influential car stylist the world has ever seen.

In 1931, in the aftermath of the Wall Street Crash of 1929, the Chevrolet marque took over sales leadership from Ford; except for a few isolated occasions, it has held the lead ever since. In the same year, even though every car-maker was struggling to sell its products, General Motors had Chevrolet, Buick and Pontiac in the 'top ten.' Before the end of that troubled decade those marques had been joined by Oldsmobile and the corporation was hugely profitable.

In 1941, when the Japanese bombed Pearl Harbor and America entered World War II, General Motors was building

BY the end of the 1920s, General Motors was a mature organization, controlled from a vast headquarters in Detroit. Through Chevrolet, Oldsmobile, Buick, Oakland and Cadillac it already dominated the United States market. In Europe GM had bought up Vauxhall (in Britain) and Opel (in Germany), and was set to expand.

In 1947 Chrysler produced this charismatic Town and Country model, which is remembered today as the *'woodie'. There was a huge demand during the post-war period, for new cars like this.*

40 percent of all cars made in the United States and 35 percent of cars built worldwide.

Opel was one of Germany's largest car-makers (in spite of interference from the Nazi party), while in Britain Vauxhall had shot up from nowhere to have a place firmly in the 'Big Six' of manufacturers. In that year Chevrolet became the world's first-ever marque to sell more than one million cars in a year. Sloan had become board chairman in 1937, and General Motors was the world's largest industrial complex.

Along the way there had only been one important casualty: La Salle. Unlike other marques in the General Motors line-up, La Salle had never had any tradition. It had been invented in 1927 as a 'junior Cadillac' and had always struggled to make its reputation. By the end of the 1930s it was being squeezed out by General Motors' own Buick and Cadillac lines (respectively slightly cheaper and slightly more expensive than La Salle), and in its last year only 24,130 cars (compared with 279,000 Buicks) were produced.

General Motors proved to be an astonishingly successful producer of military machinery during World War II. Not only did its factories produce tens of thousands of the general-purpose GMC trucks, but Sherman tanks, amphibious DUKWs ('Ducks'), aircraft engines, Grumman Avenger aircraft, sub-assemblies for Flying Fortress, Liberator and Super Fortess bomber, guns and ammunition.

GM car production started to expand again in the late 1940s, sometimes with nearly 50 percent of the domestic car market, and it has not faltered in the last 40 years. In yet another major expansion, the Holden car was launched in Australia in 1948 and swiftly became that country's market leader. In the 1950s GM's then-president 'Engine Charlie' Charles E Wilson coined that confident aphorism: ' What is good for the country is good for General Motors, and what is good for General Motors is good for the country.'

By this time it was such a large organization, with such a hold over the United States market, that it usually managed to impose its will on the customers rather than the other way around. During the 1960s, Chevrolet pushed up its annual sales to between two and two-and-a-half million, always well ahead of Ford. At the prestige end of the scale Cadillac

By the late 1950s, Detroit's confidence knew no bounds, and cars like the Chevrolet Impala were being sold in a variety of styles. This is a two-door 1958 model Sports Coupe.

INSET: The Chrysler 300 series of cars were faster, more sporty and better equipped than most. This 1959 300E convertible had a 413ci engine pushing out 380hp (SAE).

OPPOSITE ABOVE: *Buick was, and still is, one of the middle-range GM cars. Its 1958 Limited range included this four-door hardtop body style.*

LEFT: *The original Ford Thunderbird was a sporty two-seater, but the early 1960s types (this is a '64) were four-seaters.*

ABOVE: *The sensational Pontiac GTO of 1966 set new standards of performance. This extraordinarily powerful car had a 389ci V8, with 333hp as standard, and an option for an increase of power right up to 376hp!*

entered the 1950s selling 104,000 cars a year, entered the 1960s selling 142,000, and had nudged the quarter-million sales mark by 1970. The Cadillac, it seemed, was every ambitious American's dream purchase, and General Motors made sure that the cars were always available.

It was a big enough corporation to get away with major mistakes, such as the ill-handling, unreliable rear-engined Corvair of the 1960s. But it was also dynamic enough to allow inventive engineers like 'Bunkie' Knudsen to revitalize Pontiac, and tolerant enough to allow Chevrolet division to keep on selling small numbers of two-seater Corvettes for, initially at least, a tiny return. General Motors' styling might not have been liked by everyone, but it was usually taken as the standard by which other companies were judged.

The organization was large enough to shun publicly the use of motor sport as a marketing tool in the 1960s (but still sneaky enough to make sure that its engines found their way into successful race cars), and powerful enough to change American buyers' ideas by starting a downsizing program before the market asked for it. It was also bold enough to develop the idea of a 'world car' well before Ford moved the same way, with its West German subsidiary Opel often taking design leadership in such projects.

In the more practical, less jazzy 1980s, General Motors did the right thing by linking up with several Japanese manufacturers in co-design and co-production ventures, but it also misjudged the United States customers' intelligence by making its marques more and more similar. It became fashionable to mock the corporation, but its rivals were not foolish enough to write off its prospects. After 70 years of vibrantly profitable life, there is a lot still going for General Motors in the future.

FAR LEFT: *Lee Iacocca's Mustang 'pony car' was an amazing mid-1960s success. This is the '67 fastback.*

LEFT: *Chevrolet's 1967 Camaro was GM's reply to the Mustang.*

BELOW: *The Lincoln Continental Mk III was launched in 1968 as a competitor to the Cadillac – a move that proved a great success.*

Europe's Postwar Recovery

Rebuilding a shattered industry

I N May 1945, at the end of World War II in Europe, factories all over the continent lay in ruins. Most of the damage had been caused by bombing from the air, some by military action as the fighting swept through, and some by sabotage. It was going to take years to get back to normal.

Because the Allied airforces had been dominant from 1943, it was the Axis factories, in Germany and Italy, that had taken the most punishment, and here the situation was desperate. When the directors of Daimler-Benz surveyed the bombed chaos they announced succinctly that the business had 'ceased to exist,' futhermore when the occupying powers came to restart work in the giant VW plant at Wolfsburg they found it two-thirds destroyed, with no power supply and no heating.

Things were almost as bad in Italy, where Fiat's huge factories in Turin had been badly knocked about, and the Alfa Romeo factories at Portello, in Milan, had also been ill-treated by enemy bombing. Except where the Allies had made special attacks on material being made for the Germans, French factories such as the Renault and Citroën plants had fared better, and in Britain the massive 'Big Six' buildings came through relatively unscathed. Saab and Volvo, in neutral Sweden, were untouched.

As every factory had been turned over to producing weapons of war, it was going to take months merely to reinstate the car-making facilities. And that was only the start of the problems. Very little new-model design and testing had been done for six years, so at first most new cars would have to be of 1939-40 design. Not that the public minded this at all, for there was a huge pent-up demand for cars and for a bit of pleasure driving, merely to get away from the oppressive atmosphere of war.

OPPOSITE BELOW: *Bristol was a new British marque, using 'borrowed' BMW engineering to get started. The chassis design is unchanged to this day.*

RIGHT: *BMW's first post-war car, the 501 saloon, was announced in 1951. This developed version, the 502, had a V8 engine.*

BELOW: *The first new post-war Mercedes-Benz was the 300 Series of 1951.*

The costs of war now had to be faced and paid off. Britain needed to build many cars, and export nearly all of them, to start paying off its debts. Germany and Italy needed to build cars just to generate work for their starving peoples. France needed to start building cars to regain its self-respect. In every case there were shortages – of materials, of energy and, in some cases, of manpower.

In 1939 Britain had the world's second-largest automobile industry, well behind that of the United States, but comfortably ahead of its European rivals. Britain built 341,000 cars in 1938, with Germany well behind at 289,000, followed by France with about 200,000.

Increasing numbers of old-style British cars were built between 1945 and 1948, with models like the Ford Anglias and Prefects, the Austins Tens and the Morris Eights taking most sales. Nearly all the new models came from smaller concerns. No one really knew how Riley managed to show their sleek RM-Series sedans so early, Jowetts their Javelin sedans, or Armstrong-Siddeley their Whitleys and Hurricanes. Either a lot of midnight oil had been burned, or some 'secret' development had been going in the black-out.

Then, in 1948, the rush began, with the modern Morris Minor and Oxford, the standard Vanguard, the Vauxhall Velox, the Austin A40, a new type of Hillman Minx, the Land-Rover, and Jaguar XK120 and Mark V all making their appearance. By 1950, MG had produced the new TD sports car, Ford had their smooth new Consuls and Zephyrs, Alvis had the 3-liter sedan, while the limited-production Allards, Frazer Nashes and Lea Francis models were all making their mark. In five years, British car production leapt to a figure of 523,000 vehicles a year.

It was the same story in France, where the best-selling post-war Citroën 2CV and Renault 4CV economy cars took time to arrive, where the front-wheel-drive Citroën *traction avant* range was still reaching its peak, and where pre-war 'left-overs' from Simca did well for years to come. Bugatti, on the other hand, never got going again, while the glorious French *grand routier* marques such as Talbot, Hotchkiss and Delahaye gradually faded away. France's production was, however, already up to 257,000 by 1950, but the big surge (led by cars like the Renault Dauphine and the Simca Aronde) was yet to come.

ABOVE: *The Ford Consul, unveiled in 1950, had many innovations, including unit-body structures, ohv engines, and MacPherson strut front suspension.*

TOP RIGHT: *Citroen's 2CV was technically advanced in 1948, and was still made in the late 1980s.*

CENTER RIGHT: *Renault's post-war 4CV had its engine in the tail.*

RIGHT: *The VW Beetle – designed in the 1930s – struggled into production in 1945 although the final figure is 20 million plus.*

In Italy, Fiat made almost all the cars at first – 500 Topolinos, 1100s and 1500s – with only a few sports sedans from Alfa Romeo, and the Aprilias and Ardeas from Lancia. Once Alfa's factory was back in shape, the monocoque 1900 arrived, while Fiat put new 1100s, 1400s and 1900s on sale by the early 1950s. Italy was still a poor country, so by 1950 production had recovered only slowly to 101,000.

Finally there was the miraculous rebirth of West Germany, where every one of the major car plants was reduced to rubble by 1945. At first anything that could be done to employ and feed a demoralized workforce was tackled – making bicycles, kitchen utensils, and the rebuilding of trucks.

Then the push back to prosperity began, with VW Beetle sales rising to 90,000 a year by 1950. Both Ford of Germany and Opel benefitted from American ownership and were soon back on their feet, while pre-war style Mercedes-Benz cars began to appear again in growing numbers. Astonishingly enough, Porsche started building sports cars and moved to Stuttgart in 1950. BMW, only one of whose factories was not behind the Iron Curtain in East Germany, was hit hardest of all, but even so introduced the new 501 sedan for the 1950s.

West German production was only up to 214,000 by 1950, but it was to exceed British efforts by 1955 and pass the million mark a year later. By 1960 no fewer than 1.8 million cars were produced in a year. There was no doubt that the economic miracle had become economic fact.

LEFT: *For a few years, super-economy 'bubble' cars were popular in postwar Europe. Here rally driver Nancy Mitchell tries a BMW Isetta for size.*

BELOW: *To celebrate its postwar rebirth, Mercedes-Benz produced the 300SL 'gull-wing' coupe in 1954, with an amazing 150mph maximum speed.*

Chevrolet's Corvette

America's most famous sports car

AS Detroit's automobile industry got bigger and bigger, its car-makers concentrated on making the cars that sold well – sedans, convertibles and station wagons. For many years there was no time, no space and seemingly no demand, for any American company to build a sports car. Until 1953, that is, when Chevrolet took the plunge and introduced the Corvette.

For well over 30 years the Corvette has been America's most famous, and most successful, sports car. For most of that time it has in fact been the only two-seater built in North America, and it has now carved out its own niche in history.

It was not only a miracle that Detroit should announce a sports car in 1953, but that it should be badged as a Chevrolet. To tens of millions of Americans, a Chevy was the United States' best-known, most conventional and most predictable family car. Of all the companies that might possibly produce a sports car at that time, Chevrolet was certainly not the favorite.

The story began in 1952, when Chevrolet set out to produce a show car for General Motors' Motorama travelling exhibition which had been running since 1948. To make a prototype quickly and easily, they produced a new box-section chassis, but all the running gear was lifted from other existing Chevrolets and the body was molded in GRP, or glass-fiber, a newfangled material that could be shaped with the aid of cheap molds. The styling, inspired by Harley Earl, featured recessed headlamps, a wide front grille and vestigial tail-lamp fins. There were side-curtains but no wind-up door windows, and a fully wrapped-around windshield.

Chevrolet's chief engineer, Ed Cole, liked the Motorama car so much that he approved it as a production car, and only months after the first showing examples were ready for sale.

At that time, the Corvette had a six-cylinder 3.85-liter/ 235.5CID engine that produced 150hp, and a two-speed Powerglide automatic transmission. It weighed about 2900 pounds and could reach about 107mph. It did not handle all that well, and naturally it had a typically Detroit character and standard of equipment. But it *was* a two-seater sports car, and it was a start. The first batch of 300 Corvettes was assembled at Flint, in Michigan, but before the end of

1953 the car occupied its specially constructed assembly line at the General Motors factory at St Louis, Missouri, which became its permanent home.

In the beginning, the Corvette sold very slowly indeed. Only 300 1953 models were built, followed by 3640 near-identical 1954 examples, and sales dropped back to 674 in 1955. So it was only in the nick of time that Chevrolet began to build its very first V8, for this light and efficient 4.3-liter/265CID unit was the making of the car. In 1955 it provided a 195hp engine option, the car's top speed rose toward 115/120mph, and demand picked up. The Corvette needed it, for by this time it had an important new rival in Ford's steel-bodied and crisply styled two-seater Thunderbird.

It all came right for 1956, when the second-generation Corvette appeared, with the six-cylinder engine gone for good and an all-new, more stylish body which included wind-up windows. There was an optional hardtop, a 210hp engine option, and many other desirable optional features. The body was face-lifted to have four headlamps for 1958, and more than 10,000 cars were sold for the first time in 1960. Before the end of the run in 1962, 360hp V8 engines of 5.3-liters/327CID were on offer.

Then, for 1963, came the third-generation Sting Ray models, with a new chassis, all-independent suspension, coupe and convertible body styles, and top speeds of more than 140mph with the most powerful engines. Nearly 22,000 were sold in the first year, rising to 27,000 by 1966.

Only five years on, the same chassis was retained, but the very attractive fourth-generation body style was introduced.

BELOW: *The third-generation Corvette (this is a 1963 model) had eye-catching styling.*

ABOVE: *The fourth-generation Corvette Sting Ray was built from 1967 to 1983, in many forms.*

RIGHT: *Chevrolet's Aerovette has been described as 'sinfully beautiful.' It was a further development of the Astro II theme (pictured below), was first seen in 1977 and was once considered as a new Corvette for the 1980s but was dropped in 1978.*

BELOW: *The Astro II (or XP880) was a Chevrolet project car, first shown in 1968 with a mid-engined chassis layout. Later developments, known as the XP882, were also considered as new Corvettes but never put into production.*

For 1968 it was called 'Sting Ray', but 'Stingray' took over thereafter. Coupe and convertible styles were available, with lines somewhat reminiscent of the latest Ferrari Supercars (and that is exactly the impression Chevrolet wanted to give). The chassis had disc brakes all round, and engines of up to 7 liters/427CID were on offer. The most powerful engines of all had 435hp, but as United States exhaust emission laws bit deeper and deeper the large and powerful options gradually faded away.

The fourth-generation model was built from the end of 1967 until the beginning of 1983, gradually losing its character and its performance, and gradually putting on weight, as legislation tightened around it. Compulsory '5mph' bumpers were skilfully blended into the style from 1973, a coupe body derivative followed for 1978, and front and rear aerodynamic spoilers were added for 1980. Yet sales increased up and up, with nearly 54,000 vehicles being built in the peak production year of 1979.

The sensationally beautiful fifth-generation Corvette arrived during 1983, with a completely new backbone chassis, suspension, steering and glassback body style. Except that the ride was bone-shatteringly hard in Gymkhana trim, the handling was sports car-like in every way — much better than that of any other American car. By this time the V8 engine was a 5.7 liter/350CID size, with 205hp (net), which still made it one of the fastest cars on American roads, for it had a top speed of 142mph, even though fuel consumption was usually about 18 miles per gallon.

This, however, was only the beginning. More powerful engines and a fully convertible body derivative were produced in the next two or three years. The Corvette was as popular as ever, still attracting red-blooded American motorists in large numbers. It will continue to do so for many more years.

OPPOSITE: *The latest, stunningly beautiful Corvette was put on sale in 1983.*

ABOVE: *The 1967-1983 Corvettes were built as* convertibles or coupes, some with fastbacks and some with long noses . . .

BELOW: *Mean machine, a 1984 example of the modern Corvette.*

The Japanese Threat

First you copy, then you innovate

BY the mid-1980s, Japan was building eight million cars every year, which put it on a par with the United States. Its largest manufacturer, Toyota, was producing more than two-and-a-half million cars a year, making it the world's most successful single marque.

But what a change in less than 50 years. Even as recently as 1955, Japan was building only 20,000 cars in a year. The rise since then has been spectacular.

Although a few cars were built in Japan before 1941 – principally the early Toyotas (called Toyopets) and the original Austin-based Datsuns – the war put an end to all that, and by the summer of 1945 Japan's entire industry had been smashed by American bombing.

The US administration in Japan, headed by General Douglas MacArthur, then took over the running of the country. Private car production was disallowed until 1947, when a mere 300 cars were authorized. In the early post-war years the accent was on rebuilding Japan in every way, which meant that truck production took precedence. Ten years after the two atom bombs dropped in Japan had enforced peace, the 20,000 cars produced were matched by no fewer than 50,000 trucks.

In view of what was to follow, the tiny export figures are also important: only 46 cars were shipped overseas in 1956, and only 410 in 1957. Today, of course, three-and-a-half million Japanese cars are exported every year and millions more are produced in overseas factories in countries as far-flung as the United States, Britain, India, Malaysia and Australia.

There was, of course, no lengthy engineering tradition in Japan when the few pioneers began to look at the automobile market. It was with smart and advanced-design motor cycles, in fact, that Japanese companies first made their mark. By comparison, the first cars to be exported were very dull and mostly copied from one European make or another.

In the late 1950s, three European cars were being assembled in Japan. Isuzu built the Hillman Minx, by agreement with Rootes, Nissan built the Austin A50, by agreement with BMC, while Renault had licensed Hino to produce rear-engined 4CV saloons. At this time the only 'domestic' Datsun was the stubby little 1000, while Toyota were building dreadfully dull Coronas and Crowns.

The massive expansion and modernization started at the beginning of the 1960s when several new domestic cars were introduced, and Japanese engineers began to develop their own ideas for the future. At first the new Japanese cars lagged behind their European equivalents in styling, in engineering, in performance, and in road behavior, but they

ABOVE: *After making its name with motorcycles, Honda began building cars. Its very first four-wheeler (early 1960s) was this neat twin-cam, two-seater sports car. The definitive version was the S800, with a 95mph top speed.*

RIGHT: *The second Honda model, announced in 1966, was the N360/N600 mini-car, which had an air-cooled engine and front-wheel-drive. It was, however, too slow and too noisy to sell well in export markets.*

OPPOSITE: *In the 1980s Nissan became one of the world's largest car makers, but in the mid-1930s this dumpy little Datsun, based on the British Austin Seven, represented the cutting edge of Japanese car design.*

were usually well made and very reliable in service. The crowded streets of Tokyo, and the general economic conditions prevailing in Japan, meant that several of the new models were tiny and quite unsuitable for sales in other countries.

Quite suddenly, Nissan/Datsun and Toyota had competition. Mitsubishi produced its tiny 500 model in 1959, Mazda produced the little R360 in 1960, and Isuzu built its first Bellels in 1961. Most significantly, Honda, who were already noted for their motor cycles, announced the new S360/S500 sports car in 1962.

By the mid-1960s, however, the Japanese had started building larger-engined, more spacious and more conventional cars. It was these models – the Toyota Coronas and the Datsun Bluebirds, for instance – which made their mark overseas. Expansion was steady, if not spectacular, at first.

Japan's automobile industry was nowhere in 1955, eighth in the world in 1960, and sixth in 1966. Between 1967 and 1968 production rose from 1.4 million to two million, passing that of Great Britain, Italy and France along the way.

Then, as the 1970s opened, excitingly styled cars like the Datsun 240Z coupe, technically advanced cars like the Wankel-engined Mazdas and versatile machines like the Toyota Land Cruiser four-wheel-drive models came on to the scene. The Datsun Cherry started a wholesale switch to front-wheel-drive, while the Honda Civic became the first practical family car produced by that concern. These were all more attractive to overseas customers, with the result that sales spurted upward once again.

In 1971 Japanese production soared to 3.7 million, above that of West Germany. In a generation the Japanese had risen to have the world's second largest automobile industry.

ABOVE: *The Datsun 240Z went on sale in 1970 as a fast, six-cylinder, 2.4-liter coupe, with all-independent suspension. American sports car buffs loved it — more than 50,000 a year were sold in the States in mid-1970s.*

RIGHT: *The Toyota 2000GT was a real rarity, with styling influenced by a US-based German, and engine design by Yamaha. Only 337 cars were built from 1967 to 1970.*

OPPOSITE: *Mazda was the only Japanese manufacturer to adopt Wankel rotary engines. The twin-rotor RX7 sports coupe was launched in 1978, and proved very popular in the United States.*

It was no wonder that other manufacturers, the Americans in particular, hastened to forge links with the Japanese. Ford tied up with Mazda, General Motors with Isuzu, Chrysler with Mitsubishi, and eventually British Leyland got together with Honda. Toyota and Nissan later engaged in cooperative projects with General Motors. Along the way, Japanese cars built up a formidable reputation for reliability, for practicality, and — finally — for innovation. By the 1970s the Japanese could no longer be called imitators.

Although their cars still had recognizable touches of the United States in their lines, their chassis and running gear were becoming advanced and efficient.

It was the Japanese who so successfully met the demands of United States exhaust emissions legislation, the Japanese who made such advances in electronic controls, and the Japanese who cracked the problem of four-wheel steering. No wonder, therefore, that by the 1980s they vied for world leadership with the American makers.

Ferdinand Porsche

The world's best designer?

WHAT does the Porsche name mean to you? Does it identify the famous West German sports coupes? Or does it also remind you of that famous personality who had already designed many other famous machines before the cars bearing his own name even took to the street?

Dr Ferdinand Porsche had a remarkable career, remaining at the forefront of automobile design for more than 40 years. His most striking designs were those completed in the 1920s and 1930s, for all had features that we still think of as modern in the 1980s. Not many other engineers were dreaming up engines with overhead camshafts in the 1920s, mid-engined Grand Prix cars in the 1930s, or rear-engined

'people's cars' in the 1930s. Many years after its founder's death in 1951, the famous company Dr. Ing. h.c. Ferdinand Porsche GmbH has evolved into one of the world's most famous, and capable, automotive technical centers.

Ferdinand Porsche was born in 1871, in Maffersdorf, Austria-Hungary, the third child of the village tinsmith. After an apprenticeship with his father, he studied at Vienna's Technical University, then joined a local coach-building concern owned by Jacob Lohner. From there it was but a short step to designing cars, and the first Porsche-designed machine was the electric-powered Lohner-Porsche of 1900. Then, as later, he was an innovative and ruthlessly logical engineer who rarely copied another designer's ideas.

Five years later he moved to Austro-Daimler, and it was here that his love of sports cars and competition driving first became clear. In the next 30 years he was to occupy a succession of important and powerful technical positions, and to design cars as different as the VW Beetle and the supercharged Mercedes-Benz SSK sports car. Yet it was not until the 1930s that he actually controlled the destinies of his own concern.

His first-ever conventional gasoline-powered car was designed in 1909, and from this the successful Prince Henry Austro-Daimler of 1910 was born. He then went on to design gun tractors and a whole variety of military hardware in World War I, followed by more racing Austro-Daimlers in the early 1920s, before moving to Stuttgart in Germany to run the Mercedes design office in 1922.

Here Porsche built a large villa and settled down to live, for most of this work in the next 25 years was to be centered on this city. In only a few years, a whole series of supercharged sports cars and tourers was launched by Mercedes (which became Mercedes-Benz when Daimler and Benz merged in

LEFT: *Porsche's Austro-Daimler designs were very successful in motorsport. This was the original 'Prince Henry' model of 1910 which did much to establish his own and the company's name.*

TOP RIGHT: *Dr Ferdinand Porsche (1871-1951), the Austrian-born engineer who designed so many famous machines. His name lives on in the famous line of West German sports cars, although, in fact, he had little to do with their design.*

RIGHT: *British motor racing fashions of 1920 – this was G. Foresti at the wheel of an Austro-Daimler at the Brooklands race track. Note the gear lever outside the bodywork and the chain drive transmission.*

1926), all of them to Porsche's credit. These were the K, S, SS, SSK and SSKl models. However, there was more sporting prestige than profit in these cars, and when Daimler-Benz's directors asked Porsche to start designing cheap conventional cars instead, he stormed out of his job, briefly moving back to Austria to work for Steyr.

Steyr gave Porsche his head, so it was no surprise to see a large new luxury car from that stable, with a 5.3-liter eight-cylinder engine. But although this made a great impression when launched in 1929, it coincided with the great Depression. Steyr's finances collapsed, a merger with Austro-Daimler was essential, and Porsche was once again out of a job.

By this time he was fed up with working for other people, so he moved back to Stuttgart, gathered a small team of Austrian engineers around him and set up his own design consultancy business. At first he was asked to design a succession of 'people's cars' for Wanderer, NSU and Zündapp, none of which was put into production.

At about the same time, however, the Soviet government invited him to oversee *all* future Russian vehicle design and production (he was too much in love with the good life to enjoy this prospect and turned it down). Also, Auto-Union asked him to design a Grand Prix car for the new '750kg' formula of 1934; this was the very successful P-Wagen, used between 1934 and 1937.

His crowning achievement of the 1930s, however, was the 'Volkswagen' (People's Car) or KdF project for Adolf Hitler's Nazi party, which was a natural development of the Zündapp and NSU prototypes, and which was eventually to go on sale after World War II as the VW Beetle. This was about as unconventional as possible by the standards of the day, for its engine was mounted at the rear and was an air-cooled flat four, the body shape was wind-cheating rather than stylish,

LEFT: *Porsche designed a line of supercharged sports cars for Mercedes-Benz. This is the SSK version.*

LEFT INSET: *Inspired by Ferdinand Porsche, and carrying his name, the Type 356 Porsche.*

TOP: *The original 16-cylinder mid-engined Auto Union GP car of 1934 was a Porsche design.*

ABOVE: *The Porsche-designed 'people's car' became the Hitler-sponsored VW Beetle.*

and the all-independent suspension was designed for cheapness and ride comfort rather then good roadholding. It was also a high-geared car, capable of being cruised flat-out on Germany's new motor roads, and Hitler originally demanded that it should sell for a mere 1000 Reichmarks (£90).

Its importance to the future Porsche company can be seen from the fact that the first Porsche sports car (in which the famous designer was not personally involved) used the underpan and running gear of the VW Beetle. . .

As well as concentrating most of his efforts on the VW project in the next few years, Porsche also found time to design the Type T80 Mercedes-Benz land speed record contender (which was still not complete when war broke out). During the war he was responsible for several important military designs.

Immediately after the war he was arrested and spent some time in prison in France. As an old man, his constitution was not up to the experience, and when he was finally released in 1947 his health had been broken. Although regularly consulted by his family, he had little to do with the design of the first Porsche 356, which entered production in 1949. He died in January 1951, but his name lives on in the charismatic Stuttgart-based Porsche company.

The Ferrari Legend

The great Italian supercar

SOME names need no explanation. Mention Christian Dior to a woman and she thinks of couture clothes. Mention Purdy to a sportsman and he thinks of the best handbuilt shotguns in the world. Mention Ferrari to *anyone*, and the response is invariably the same – that Ferrari build the fastest and finest supercars in the business.

Although Enzo Ferrari was already a well-known racing driver in the 1920s and a noted team manager in the 1930s, there were no Ferrari cars before World War II. Sales began in 1947, but only three cars were built in that year; it was not until 1957 that more than 100 Ferraris were built in one year.

Ferrari went into the car-building business as a racing enthusiast who built a few road cars, rather than the other way round. He could never be troubled to make bodies for his supercars. That situation gradually changed over the years,

for Ferrari came to control the coachbuilders Scaglietti, but even to this day no Ferrari body shell is constructed in a Ferrari factory.

In those early years, a Ferrari's excellence was centered on its magnificent engine, with the styling next in importance, and the specification of the chassis last of all. It was not until the 1960s that Ferrari's chassis design caught up with that of its rivals – but no one ever complained about the performance.

In the beginning, every Ferrari had a single-overhead-camshaft 60-degree V12 engine, which had been designed by Gioacchino Colombo. It started life as a 1.5-liter unit, but the same basic design was eventually stretched to 3.3-liters. A second V12, designed by Aurelio Lampredi, was larger and heavier. It was not until the mid-1960s that any other type of engine was fitted to a Ferrari road car.

The original Ferraris were the Inter series, which had front-mounted V12 engines, rear-wheel-drive, and simple tubular-frame chassis, with independent front suspension and beam rear axles. The same basic layout, with many permutations of engine size and power, wheelbase length, and special body style, was to be used until the mid-1960s. After the Inter came the Europa, the very exclusive America, SuperAmerica and Superfast models, and the long-running 3-liter engined 250GT family. All were assembled at Maranello, near Modena, in Italy – and all were tested and developed on the open road.

The early cars had 110hp, but all the 250GTs had 240hp or more, and the monstrous Superfasts sometimes had up to

OPPOSITE: *Enzo Ferrari (left) has been at the pulse of Grand Prix racing for more than 60 years. Here he is at Monza with Tino Brambilla in 1968.*

BELOW: *The 500 Superfast of 1964-1966 had a 400hp 5-liter V12 engine. Perhaps not surprisingly, only 37 such 170mph cars were ever built.*

LEFT INSET: *There were several different types of Ferrari 250GT, but the most famous of all was the race-proved short-wheelbase Berlinetta of the early 1960s.*

RIGHT INSET: *Until the early 1960s every Ferrari was a two-seater. Then, in 1960, the Pininfarina-styled 2×2 seat 250GTE was launched. Some 950 such cars were built.*

BELOW: *The first V8-engined Ferrari was the 308 family, introduced in 1973 and still selling today in 328 form. This is a 308GTB.*

400hp. It was no wonder that most 250GTs could approach 150mph, while the Superfasts were good for more than 170mph. The most famous of this generation were the 250GT Berlinettas and the 250GTOs which followed them, for these were beautiful cars that also won many GT races.

As production increased, a series of 'standard', but still sensationally beautiful, body styles was developed, though many one-off bodies, especially convertibles, were still produced from time to time. Standard shapes were usually by Pininfarina, though Scaglietti of Modena generally made the shells to this design.

In the meantime, Ferrari came to prominence in Grand Prix and sports car racing, began winning in the early 1950s, and have been winning ever since. It was often said that Ferrari merely built road cars to help finance his racing in the early days. This was certainly true, but by the 1960s the road cars were in great demand on their own and the one side of Ferrari helped publicize the other.

Major design changes were made to the Ferrari line-up in the mid-1960s, not only when a new chassis with all-independent suspension and a rear-mounted drive train was produced for the 275GTB, but when a completely new type of smaller, transverse mid-engined 'Dino' was put on sale.

The 275GTB retained a front-mounted V12 engine, and was later replaced by 365GTB/4 Daytona, which could reach nearly 175mph and is often said to be the world's fastest-ever front-engined road car. At first the Dino was sold without

Ferrari badges, as a 'Dino' marque (the name was that of Ferrari's son, who died in his twenties), but every Ferrari enthusiast knows it as a Ferrari. Early cars had 2.0-liter V6 engines, but a 2.4-liter engine was later fitted.

From 1969, Fiat took financial control of Ferrari (and actually built a Ferrari-engined Fiat Dino of their own at this time), which allowed Enzo Ferrari to concentrate on his beloved racing cars. It also allowed Ferrari road car production to be increased. Ferrari built more than 1000 cars in a year for the first time (1246 in fact) in 1971, and this rose rapidly to 2221 in 1979. By the mid-1980s demand had increased still further and Ferrari production was exceeding 3000 a year.

To replace the V6 engined Dinos, Ferrari then introduced a series of mid-V8 engined models in the 308 (later 328) family. More sensationally still, to replace the Daytona, the mid-flat-12 engined Berlinetta Boxer went on sale in 1974; it was in its turn replaced, 10 years later, by the even more beautiful Testarossa. A few front-engined cars, latterly the 400 and 412 four-seaters, continued, but by the 1980s Ferrari was the world leader in fearsomely fast and beautiful engineered mid-engined two-seaters and 2+2.

In 40 years, Ferrari has probably produced more new, modified, or different engines than any other company, whether for road or racing cars. A study of the many Ferrari books shows engines as small as 1.0-liter, as large as 7.0-liters, in configurations as different as the famous V12s, V6s and V8s, plus flat 12s, flat eights, straight fours, straight sixes and even, on one occasion, a parallel twin.

No other company, not even Lamborghini or Porsche, has ever produced a car with the charisma of a Ferrari, which is every schoolboy's dream. You could drool over the styling, over the engine, or even over the noise, but best of all you can always drool over the name – Ferrari!

OPPOSITE ABOVE: *The 275GTB was revealed in 1964.*

OPPOSITE BELOW: *The 308GT4 of 1973 had a mid-mounted V8 engine.*

Bertone styling, and 2+2 seating.

BELOW: *This was the original mid-V6 Dino style of 1967-1973. Most had 2.4-liter engines.*

BELOW: *Perfect for California and Hawaii, if not for Europe – the open-topped 308GTS, complete with four-cam V8 engine.*

INSET RIGHT: *The superb 365GTB/4 Daytona, with 352hp and a top speed of around 175mph is probably the world's fastest front-engined road car.*

The Magnificent XK

Jaguar's famous dual-cam engine

ALL over the world, Jaguar enthusiasts can thank Adolf Hitler for one thing – it was the Luftwaffe's efforts that led to the birth of the famous dual-overhead-camshaft XK engine. This was designed for William Lyons by his engineers while they were carrying out weekend fire-watching duties at the factory in Coventry. Chief engineer Bill Heynes, designer Claude Baily and chief development engineer Walter Hassan, were all involved.

The Jaguar's ancestor was the SS1 of 1931, and the first SS-Jaguar was announced in 1935. The 'SS' name was dropped in 1945, immediately after World War II, those initials having become hated because of their connection with Nazi Germany.

Jaguar was a small company, very prudently financed, so at first all the major mechanical items like engines and drive trains had to be bought in from the Standard company. William Lyons, though, wanted to build his own cars in his own way after the war, and was determined to produce his own

ABOVE: *Although the XK engine was not designed for racing, it was an astonishing success when fitted in Jaguar racing cars. The sleek D-Type won the 1956 Le Mans 24 Hour race.*

RIGHT: *Looking as powerful as it was then, the 265hp/4.2 liter version of the legendary XK 'six' as used in the XKE of 1965.*

LEFT AND ABOVE LEFT: *Two versions of the much-admired Jaguar XK120 coupe.*

LEFT: *Although it was heavy, the XK engine was very sturdy, which explains why it was such a good 'endurance' racing car engine. This D-type has just won the Le Mans 24 Hour race of 1956.*

RIGHT: *The XK engine was originally designed to power Jaguar's post-war saloons, and was used in the Mk 6/Mk 8/Mk 9 models.*

OVERLEAF: *The fabulous E-Type, powered by the XK engine.*

OVERLEAF INSET: *The leaping Jaguar mascot, one of the world's famous car 'trade marks.'*

BELOW: *The XK engine was fitted to the Jaguar C-type racing sports cars, which won the Le Mans 24 Hour races of 1951 and 1953, and counted Stirling Moss amongst its drivers.*

engine designs to power all of them. His brief was simple – he wanted a family of units more advanced, more refined and more powerful than any of the rival products.

As Walter Hassan later recalled: 'He was insistent on having an engine which would look smart and powerful. His new engine would have to be good-looking, with all the glamor of the famous engines produced for racing in previous years, so that when you opened the hood of a post-war Jaguar you would be looking at power and be impressed.'

Design work centered on a family of four-cylinder and six-cylinder engines, which would share a lot of common parts and would be machined on the same tools. Although all engines sold to the public were straight sixes, all the early work was concentrated on the smaller straight fours.

The very first prototype design was the XF, a 1.36-liter four, with dual-overhead-camshaft valve gear, but the second was the 1.76-liter XG, which had a side-camshaft and BMW-like cross-pushrod valve gear. Then came the XJ design, which featured light-alloy cylinder heads with part-spherical combustion chambers, and dual overhead camshafts driven by chain; there were 2-liter four-cylinder and 3.2-liter six-cylinder versions of this design at first. The first XJs ran in 1946, but by 1948 they had evolved into XK units, with longer strokes and even more torque than before.

The new engines were revealed in 1948 when both types – four-cylinder and six-cylinder – were supposed to be fitted to strikingly styled new two-seater sports cars called XK100 and XK120. As we now know, the four-cylinder engine was never put into production, but the six-cylinder unit was built continuously until 1986. For a time, the Jaguar engine was the only series-production twin-cam in the world, and most subsequent designs copied some its features.

The six-cylinder XK engine did everything Lyons had asked his designers to achieve. It was very powerful, it was very refined, and it looked absolutely magnificent. There were several bonuses, too. It was a very docile, flexible engine which was silky smooth and ideal for use in sports cars, sedans and racing cars alike. It was also very strong and

longlived. Although early examples tended to be oil-leakers (a problem which was later cleared up by the development engineers), XK engines were soon renowned for the way they kept going.

At first, every XK engine built was a six-cylinder, 3.4-liter, 160hp unit, as used in the XK120 and XK140 sports cars and the Mark VII sedan. Shortly Jaguar began to use it in racing sports cars, such as the XK120C (which won at Le Mans in 1951 and 1953) and the D-Type (winner at Le Mans on three further occasions). This resulted in several other independent race-car manufacturers queueing up to buy engines for their own cars.

In the mid-1950s a number of different engine sizes were also developed. On the one hand there was an enlarged 3.8-liter unit (first for racing, then for production cars), and on the other there was the smaller 2.4-liter size (for the compact sedan of that name introduced in 1955).

Next, the pressure of racing saw prototype 3.0-liter sizes produced, different cylinder-head castings evolved, and aluminum cylinder blocks successfully tested. Engines with four valves per cylinder were drawn up, but they were never built.

By the early 1960s there was pressure for even more powerful road-car engines, even through the original 3.8-liter XKE of 1961 had 265hp. So in 1964 the XK engine was stretched to its limit, 4.2-liters, this size then being offered in the latest XKE sports cars, in the Mark 10 sedans and, eventually, in the 420 sedans.

Even after 20 years of life the XK engine's career was not over. When the sensational XJ6 sedans was launched in 1968, Jaguar made no secret of the fact a new V12 engine was being developed for that car, but the XK engine – in 2.8, 3.4 and 4.2-liters sizes – still powered the vast majority of all the cars produced.

It was not until 1983 that Jaguar announced the first of the new family of six-cylinder engines – the AJ6 units – and even then the venerable XK engine was to carry on for another three years. In a 38-year career, it was not only used in hundreds of thousands of Jaguar (and Daimler) passenger cars, but it also found its way into Alvis armored fighting vehicles, into power boats, and into single-seater racing cars. Power outputs ranged from the 112hp 2.4-liter size to more than 340hp in the best and most highly tuned race car installation.

RIGHT: *Starting with the 2.4 of 1955, a series of 'compact' XK-powered Jaguars were built over the next 14 years. Every one was powered by the six-cylinder dual-cam Jaguar XK engine.*

BELOW: *Three versions of the XK engine – 2.8, 3.4, and 4.2-liter – were used in the long-running XJ6 series, built in Britain from 1968 to 1987.*

Very Exclusive Cars

For very exclusive customers

N O matter how hard the economic climate, the rich will always be rich. If more of us knew why, perhaps more of us would be rich. Ah, well. . .

In automobile industry terms, this means that there will always be a sale, if only a restricted sale, for truly dignified and exclusive cars from Rolls-Royce, Bentley, Hispano-Suiza and Mercedes-Benz. Not Supercars, you understand, and not outrageously styled monstrosities, but cars for gentlemen and their families. It is a market, however, which is almost impossible to broach, unless there is a lot of tradition to back up that attempt.

By the 1930s, the four cars already named had sliced up the market between them as most other cars faded away. Pierce-Arrow and Marmon were killed off by the Depression and its after-effects. Bugatti was not in the business of building refined and practical road cars, Isotta-Fraschini was well past its best days, while Cadillac and Lincoln had both gone for quantity, instead of limited-production quality, sales.

RIGHT: *The Duesenberg J was introduced in 1928, and produced until the mid 1930s. The customer could specify any type of body-work on the car's 200hp chassis – this Rollston-bodied Victoria was delivered in 1931.*

BELOW: *Duesenberg built the most powerful American car of the early 1930s – the 320hp supercharged eight-cylinder SJ model. This was so costly that only 36 cars were ever built.*

The British Daimler concern, though still building sleeve-valve engined cars, and continuing to supply the British royal family with its limousines, was also steadily moving down market.

Hispano-Suiza was the first to abandon automobile manufacture for 'top people', in 1938, after a glittering period between the wars. There were two outstanding Hispanos: the six-cylinder H6B model introduced in 1919, at the time the most advanced in the world, and the magnificent V12 model of 1931-38 which was faster, grander and more imposing than any other car of its day. Only if you had the pleasure of driving behind that splendid 9.4-liter engine, perhaps swathed in a Saoutchick, Binder, or Letourner et Marchand body shell, did you know for sure that no one else, king or tycoon, could surpass you on the day!

Even though Mercedes-Benz made more and more small-engined family cars in the 1930s-50s period, and had to recover from being obliterated by bombing in World War II, it still made a few truly remarkable top-of-the-range cars. In the 1930s there were two different types of Grosser model — both with supercharged straight eight-cylinder engines. The first was an old-fashioned car with hard springing, but the

1938-39 variety had an advanced chassis, gargantuan eight-seater body, and was mostly sold to Nazi leaders who found its impressive size to their liking.

The modern 'Grosser,' however, was the angularly styled 600 range introduced in 1963, which was even more technically advanced than the Rolls-Royce Silver Shadow with which it had to compete. You simply *had* to be a 'top person' to afford a car that had self-levelling suspension, power-operated everything, a 6.3-liter engine, and was so long and heavy that it helped to have acres of parking space wherever you stopped.

After Rolls-Royce bought up the bankrupt remains of Bentley in 1931 (some say, to kill off the excellent 8-liter, others so that they could take control of the famous Le Mans-winning marque's reputation), it really had the lion's share of all top-drawer car sales, a happy situation that the company has held to this day.

A new Bentley, based on Rolls-Royce components, was announced in 1933, and for the next two decades the Bentley was marketed as a sporting car ('The Silent Sports Car' was its advertising slogan), while the Rolls-Royce was marketed as 'The Best Car in the World.'

Until the mid-1960s, Rolls-Royce sold its products on the quality of engineering and construction, rather than on technical modernity. Only the short-lived Phantom III's V12 engine of 1935-39 was ahead of its notional rivals. Components such as servo-brakes (after Hispano-Suiza), synchromesh transmission (General Motors), coil-spring independent front suspension (Packard, in particular), and the V8 engine (Chrysler and Cadillac especially) were all seen on other cars before 'The Best Car. . .' adopted them.

The feature that really sold the Rolls-Royce and Bentley marques to wealthy customers was the quality, exclusivity and style of the coachwork. Until 1939, the cars were all supplied as rolling chassis to coachbuilders, who had taken the individual orders from the customers and built bodies to suit. Most of these had wooden framing and hand-beaten or rolled skin panels.

Rolls-Royce introduced factory-designed 'standard steel bodies' on Bentleys from 1946, and on Rolls-Royce Silver Dawns from 1949. However, all the post-war Phantoms (the very rare IV and the more numerous Vs and VIs) have special coachbuilt shells, as did the mouth-watering selection of Bentley Continentals built from 1952 on. Since the standard

In Europe in the 1930s, if you were truly rich – and discerning – you might buy a V12 Hispano-Suiza. Without doubt this car had the best chassis in the world, and the special bodies usually matched it. The stork mascot was quite unmistakeable to all lovers of fine cars.

cars retained separate chassis until 1965 it was quite usual to see special coachwork on these cars too.

From 1946 to 1965, the technical specification of Rolls-Royce cars gradually fell behind the times, for components like drum brakes were kept during that period. However, from 1966 the Silver Shadow models (and their Bentley T-Series equivalents) took over, combining typical Rolls-Royce quality and the usual patrician radiator style with a much lower monocoque shell, self-levelling suspension, disc brakes, full-power hydraulics, a V8 engine and automatic transmission.

It is a recipe that clearly appealed to the customer, for sales gradually increased to more than 3000 cars a year. There seems to be no likelihood of the 'Best Car in the World' losing its attraction in the next few years.

OPPOSITE INSET: *Every Mercedes-Benz Type 600 Grosser was large and impressive, but the really large examples were the long-wheelbase Pullmans, with six passenger doors.*

BELOW: *The British coachbuilder H J Mulliner got together with Bentley to produce the R-Type Continental in 1952. It was sleek, graceful – and very fast.*

Front-Wheel-Drive!

The Mini changes the face of motoring

LOOK around you today, and you will see that growing numbers of the world's modern small cars have front engines, transversely mounted, with front-wheel-drive. There has to be a pioneer for every trend, and in this case it is all down to one man and one car. The man was Alec Issigonis, and the car was the BMC Mini.

There was nothing brand new about the layout of the Mini when it was launched in 1959, but Issigonis' small team of engineers had packaged it all in an extraordinarily compact, effective and appealing manner. Front-wheel-drive, after all, had first been seen on a car in the early 1900s, while there was nothing at all new about transversely mounted engines.

The Mini had all-independent suspension, but this was well known, and it had rack-and-pinion steering, but this was already in use in several other cars. It was merely that the Mini packaged a whole combination of features so much better than had ever been done before.

In previous generations, small cars had merely been smaller versions of large cars, and they tended to use the same basic design. They were merely smaller in all dimensions, with less passenger space and less performance; the engine was still at the front and the driven wheels were still at the rear. As the cars shrank, so did the passenger space.

Then, after World War II, European designers led the way with some very advanced small cars. Renault produced the rear-engined/rear-drive 4CV model, Citroën brought out the front-engined/front-drive 2CV, the air-cooled rear-engined VW Beetle went on sale, and Fiat eventually produced the rear-engined/rear-drive 600 model.

Alec Issigonis had already designed the post-war Morris Minor before going off to work for Alvis for a time, and was then attracted back to BMC (which had taken over the Morris marque) to work on new small-car designs. After the Suez Crisis of 1956 and the petrol rationing that followed it, he set about creating a completely new generation of cars for BMC.

Except that he was ordered to use a modified version of an existing BMC engine, which meant that he had to use a water-cooled four-cylinder unit, Issigonis was given a com-

BELOW: *This was the very first 'off track' Mini, built at Longbridge in 1959.*

OPPOSITE: *Paddy Hopkirk winning the 1968 Monte*

Carlo Rally.

OPPOSITE INSET: *The Mini's engine (this is a Mini-Cooper) was transversely mounted.*

pletely free hand. His view, quite simply, was that all the world's small cars without exception had wasted some passenger space because of styling, so he would concentrate all his efforts on improving this situation. The result was the ADO 15 project, which the world now knows as the Mini.

He decided to concentrate all the engine/drive train bulk in the same place, and to eliminate a front-to-rear drive shaft through the passenger compartment. This meant that he could mount the engine and drive train at the front, with front-wheel-drive, or at the rear, to drive the rear wheels. With weight distribution and ultimate roadholding in mind, he chose front-wheel-drive.

He also wanted to make the car as short as possible, while still being able to carry four full-sized adults. His stroke of genius, therefore, was to turn the engine sideways and mount it transversely, lift it slightly, and place the main transmission under it, in the sump. Instead of being at the front, the cooling radiator was to one side of the engine bay, drawing its air through holes in the left-side fender well.

Next he decided that as conventional-sized fender wells always intruded on passenger space, he would cut down the wheel size dramatically. The Mini became the first British car ever to use 10-inch diameter wheels. The suspension was also very compactly laid out, with trailing arms at the rear.

The result was that the whole package was squeezed into an overall length of 10 feet and a width of 4 feet 7½ inches, and the unladen weight was a mere 1340 pounds. However, because the 848cc engine produced 34hp, the Mini had a brisk performance and a top speed of nearly 75mph. Alec Issigonis gleefully claimed that, of the 10-foot length, at least 8 feet was allocated to passengers.

OPPOSITE: *Stark-bodied Mini Mokes have been built since 1964.*

OPPOSITE, INSET: *The privately-developed Mini Sprint had lowered lines and rectangular lamps.*

BELOW: *Many designers copied the Mini layout: here, a Fiat 127.*

However, not only was the Mini tiny, but it also had astonishing roadholding, handling and stability. The steering was inch-accurate, the small car could be threaded in and out of traffic in a very nimble fashion, and on twisty country roads it was as fast as much more expensive cars. It also had lashings of that elusive feature in a car, character, which endeared it to everyone who drove it.

Within months, every rival factory in Europe had bought a Mini, studied it and stripped it out, to see what they could learn. They learned a lot – and none of it was reassuring for companies wedded to the old style of designing cars. It was not just the Mini's amazing road manners or its irrepressible character which worried the opposition, but the breakthrough in packaging that Issigonis' team had achieved.

As it stood, there was a lot wrong with the Mini that ought never to have been copied, but there was also much that was right. The Mini's rubber suspension was too hard and too expensive to produce (whereas the Hydrolastic suspension that followed it in the mid-1960s was too queasily supple); there were really too many problems in asking a transmission to share its oil with the engine; the driving position was cramped; and the trunk was really far too small.

On the other hand, the amount of passenger space was incredibly generous for such a small car, and the behavior of the front-wheel-drive chassis was quite faultless. With a bit more money spent on quality control, a few more inches on length and width to improve accommodation still further, and maybe a hatchback to increase the stowage possibilities, and who knows what could be achieved?

Within three years Issigonis had extended the Mini formula with the more spacious 1100 models, and within five years the first rival cars were ready, starting with the Autobianchi Primula of 1964 and the Peugeot 204 of 1965. Once the Japanese chimed in, with cars like the little Honda N360, the trend was obvious to everyone. Nowadays, as a result of Alec Issigonis' bright ideas, front-wheel-drive and transverse engines are the norm for all compact car designs.

Unsafe at Any Speed?

The Corvair story

WHEN it was announced in the autumn of 1959, the Chevrolet Corvair caused a real stir in the world of the automobile. By the time independent testers had tried out the 1960 model its initial high reputation was already beginning to slide. After Ralph Nader's book *Unsafe at Any Speed* was published it became almost unsaleable. Yet the Corvair was neither as bad, nor as good, as was stated. What was it all about, and what went wrong?

The Corvair was conceived in the mid-1950s, at a time when all of Detroit's 'Big Three' – Ford, Chrysler and Chevrolet – turned to what became known as the compact car. Three new cars, one from each group, were launched in 1959; even though they were compacts, they were all six-seaters. The difference, however, was that Ford and Chrysler designed conventional front-engine/rear-drive cars, whereas Chevrolet produced a very way-out machine indeed. It was not coincidence that the ugly but reliable VW Beetle was at the height of its reputation in the United States, or that the General Motors line was currently very staid and in need of a shake-up.

Led by its adventurous chief engineer, Ed Cole, the Chevrolet design team not only conceived a sporty compact car, but one that aped many things that had worked so well for VW. The new model, which was eventually given the name 'Corvair', was completely different from any previous Chevrolet – and different, indeed, from any previous American car.

Like the VW Beetle, the Corvair was given an air-cooled engine, mounted at the rear, along with both independent front and rear suspension. Because of the restrictions on available space, the back end was a simple swing-axle design, and more than half of the car's weight was over those rear wheels.

Unlike the Beetle, however, the Corvair was given a 2.3-liter flat six engine, in 80hp or 95hp tune; allegedly this was inspired by Ed Cole's interest in light aircraft. Unlike the Beetle it was offered with a choice of three-speed or four-speed manual transmission, or with two-speed automatic transmission. Its kerb-side weight was about 2400 pounds, creditable by other General Motors' cars' standards, but at least 100 pounds more (all at the back end) than Ed Cole had hoped.

The other major technical innovation was that it was the very first Chevrolet to have a unit-construction body/chassis design, this being engineered around an easily recognizable body style, with what became known as a 'bathtub' ridge around the waistline. In the current fashion then prevailing in the United States, it had four circular headlamps. Two-door or four-door sedans and a four-door station wagon were all offered on the same chassis. Incidentally, it was a triumph of packaging that a rear-mounted engine and rear-loading station wagon body could both be found on the same car; even VW was impressed.

At first it was sold as the 700 Series (cheap), or 500 Series (very cheap), though in 1960 a more upmarket version, the 900 Monza, came along with bucket seats and a two-door coupe style.

The Corvair's problem was that it handled like no American car had ever handled before. All other current models understeered, whereas the Corvair felt much more 'nervous' and oversteered. It needed much lower front than rear tire pressures even to feel safe, and there was always the possibility that the tail would try to overtake the front in hard cornering or wet road maneuvering. Very few run-of-the-mill American drivers could cope with this – nor many journalist testers. It was not until 1962 that Chevrolet offered a stiffer handling package, and not until 1964 that a transverse compensating spring was fitted to help cut down rear-wheel tuck-under.

ABOVE: *Chevrolet's Corvair was completely different from every other American car. Its engine was in the tail, and was an air-cooled flat-six.*

RIGHT: *The Corvair had all-independent suspension, and 'bath-tub' styling.*

LEFT INSET: *One of several experimental Chevrolet Corvairs not sold to the public – the Sebring Spyder of 1961.*

BELOW INSET *GM's glossy advertising promised all manner of fun in the Corvair. This was the 1962 Monza Convertible, more powerful and more fun to use than the saloons.*

RIGHT INSET: *Even though the Corvair Sebring Spyder looked very sporty, it still had the air-cooled engine at the back, and somewhat perilous handling characteristics.*

Even though there was criticism of the Corvair's handling and of the quality of its construction, Chevrolet went out for the sports-car market in the next few years. Monzas eclipsed the sedans, while the station wagons sold only slowly. More powerful engines came along, as did a convertible called the Monza Spider, and GM even became world-leaders by introducing a turbocharged engine option on the most upmarket version.

Enter Ralph Nader, a young crusader trained in the law, who took up consumer matters, with automobile safety as his speciality. By 1964 he had homed in on General Motors' overall attitude to safety, and in particular their lack of progress with the Corvair. His celebrated book, *Unsafe at Any Speed*, put the skids under a car that was already well past its peak, and not even the launch of a radically improved Corvair for 1965 could stem the tide.

The 1965 Corvair had much better chassis, with wishbone rear suspension, and there was a Corsa model with 140 or 180hp which took over from the Monza Spider. In 180hp form this Corvair could reach 115mph and run with the best of British sports cars. Not only that, but there was a smooth new body style, with a more flowing fender line, and altogether better trimmed interiors.

It was a great car, but it was all too late. The GM Board had already taken the decision to let the Corvair project wind itself down, so the 209,000 cars in 1965 slumped to 86,000 in 1966, and to a mere 12,887 in 1968. About 1.5 million Corvairs had been sold before the directors had clashed with Ralph Nader in open court proceedings, and just 125,000 thereafter. In May 1969 they announced that Ed Cole's dream car was to be killed off, and there was no 1970 model.

It would be a long time before General Motors was so adventurous again.

Wankel's Engine

Whatever happened to the rotary engine?

IF the Man from Mars landed on earth tomorrow, no doubt he would be amused by the archaic engines used on most of the world's cars. For aircraft, ships and many types of railway locomotive, power is provided by pure rotary engines. But for cars there are the crudities of converting reciprocating piston movements into the rotary movement of a crankshaft. Clearly, he would say, these Earthlings have got it all wrong − if pure rotary power works for their large transport machines, why not for cars?

Perhaps if Otto's reciprocating engine had not been the first to develop, and had not worked tolerably well right from the start, it might never had made it to the first centenary of

ABOVE RIGHT: *Dr Felix Wankel poses proudly behind an early example of the famous rotary engine which bears his name. The rotor tip seals which caused so many problems are clearly visible.*

RIGHT: *The first Wankel-engined car to be put on sale was the NSU Spider of 1964, which had a single-rotor engine mounted in the tail.*

OPPOSITE ABOVE: *This was the book which effectively killed off the Corvair, and did great harm to GM's corporate image. Even so, the late-model Corvairs were fine-handling machines.*

OPPOSITE: *Here is another GM Corvair project car of 1964, the Monza, again never put on sale. Its easy to see where the mid-engined Corvette styles of the late 1960s came from.*

the automobile. Perhaps it is only habit that keeps the world building car engines this way? Or is it?

Until gas-turbine aero-engines were invented in the 1930s, and brought into military and commercial service in the 1950s, there was no alternative – though man the inventor often tried to find a better way. Surely there *had* to be a better way?

Dr Felix Wankel (like his illustrious predecessors, Otto and Diesel, also a German-born engineer) thought he had the answer. Like most of his peers he realized that scaling down the dimensions of gas-turbine engines was always going to be incredibly difficult and expensive, so he set about designing a different type of rotary.

The Wankel engine, as it became known, used the idea of a specially shaped rotor revolving inside a chamber of even more specialized shape; the rotor needed an eccentric shaft (a crankshaft, really) to give it the appropriate movement. In that way, a fuel/air mixture could be sucked in, compressed, exploded, and expelled from the annular spaces formed between rotor and chamber, therefore producing power. It was not pure rotary power, but it was a start.

The original engines of the 1950s were single-rotor units, which felt unbalanced and suffered from all manner of problems. Yet NSU, of West Germany, were interested, worked together with Wankel, and eventually put the world's first Wankel-engined car, the two-seat Wankel Spider, on sale in 1964. It was a pretty little car, with the engine mounted in the tail, and from a (nominal) 500cc engine which produced 50hp, it had a top speed of around 90mph.

The problem for NSU was twofold. To make such engines in volume, an entirely new generation of precision machine tools had to be designed, financed and installed. To make the

engines reliable, a mountain of work was needed on the tip that separated the rotors from the chambers.

The pundits, and in small numbers the public, were impressed, so NSU took a deep breath and went to the next stage. In 1967 it launched the futuristic Ro80 sedan model,

OPPOSITE: *In 1969 Mercedes-Benz announced the triple-rotor C-111 research project.*

OPPOSITE, INSET: *The Wankel-powered C-111 had its engine behind the seats, and used gull-wing doors.*

ABOVE: *The NSU Wankel Spider, was the first Wankel-powered car.*

BELOW: *The NSU Ro80 of 1967 had a twin-rotor engine.*

in which there was a 105hp *twin*-rotor Wankel engine. This gave the car sports sedan performance, was smoother and quieter than the original, seemed capable of unlimited engine revs, and was a very attractive proposition.

Except that it was still very unreliable, and very expensive to build. All over Europe, Ro80 engines blew up after 10-20,000 miles of high-speed life and cost a fortune to be replaced. NSU struggled on with development, balanced its costs as well as it could, but eventually had to merge with VW. It was the beginning of the end for this branch of the Wankel engine.

In the meantime, Wankel development was breaking out all around the world. In West Germany Daimler-Benz started testing, as did Rolls-Royce in Britain, while Citroën came to a coproduction agreement with NSU. In the United States, not only Curtiss-Wright (who built aero-engines), but General Motors took out licenses, while in Japan it was Toyo Kogyo (whose cars were sold with Mazda badges) which took up the challenge.

Wankel fever was at its height at the end of the 1960s. Not only had Mercedes-Benz shown the impressive triple-rotor C111 mid-engined project car, which looked, and was, as fast as any racing sports car in the world, but Mazda's first Wankel-engined car, the 110S Cosmo coupe, had been put on sale, closely followed by several others. The mighty General

Motors announced that its own Wankel-engined cars would be launched on the market by 1974.

Unhappily for Wankel himself, the big breakthrough never came. Costs of engines, and cars fitted with them, remained high, and the bad publicity of premature failure could not be hidden. The public became suspicious when firms like Rolls-Royce and Mercedes-Benz tested and tested, but never brought themselves to put Wankel-engined products on sale.

When compared directly with their rivals, it was found that Wankel engines were not as fuel-efficient, and engineers also discovered that it was very difficult for a Wankel engine to meet the increasingly severe exhaust emission laws which the world's legislators were pushing through and for this latter reason it was dropped by GM and Ford. Only Mazda persevered, for by 1973 they had four such cars – R100, RX2, RX3 and RX4 – on the market.

Then, in 1973-74, the bottom dropped out of the market. Israel clashed with Egypt in the Middle East, the Organization of Petroleum Exporting Countries (OPEC) dramatically pushed up the price of crude oil, and the days of cheap gasoline supplies were over for ever. Mazda's sales of rotary-engined cars plunged and General Motors abandoned their production program. NSU phased out the Ro80, and every other research program was slashed.

In the end, only Mazda stayed the course. It made dramatic improvements in reliability, fuel-efficiency and the level of exhaust emissions, and announced the fast and attractive Wankel-engined RX7 coupe in 1978, of which eventually hundreds of thousands were sold. A new generation of RX7s took over in 1986, but it is still the only Wankel-engined production car in the modern world. Will it ever have a rival?

Throughout the 1970s Mazda persisted with the Wankel engine, and sold hundreds of thousands of RX7 sports coupes. The second-generation RX7 Savanna was launched in 1985, has 185hp, and a fast 140mph maximum speed.

Ten Million Cars Each Year

Detroit's great post-war expansion

Although it took time for Detroit to produce new post-war models, the wait was worthwhile. One of the most startling early-1950s styles came from Studebaker, courtesy of the Loewy studios.

BRITAIN'S automobile industry stopped car production almost as soon as Britain declared war on Germany in September 1939. But Detroit, in an America still at peace, carried on building cars full blast until the beginning of 1942. The production lines then turned over to making weapons of war as diverse as the Jeep and the Sherman tank, Rolls-Royce Merlin aero-engines and six-wheel-drive trucks. Nevertheless, when victory over Japan was finally achieved in August 1945, the private-car assembly lines had been closed down for less than four years.

In North America, as in Europe, there was a huge pent-up demand for private cars when the war was over. Not only had a lot of older models been worn out or crashed in the intervening four years, but the release of millions of self-confident military veterans into civilian life at that time also meant that there was a great deal of money washing around in the United States.

As in Europe, most of the early post-war American cars were pre-war designs. Some had been introduced as recently as 1941, but some were considerably older than that. No matter — the tools and facilities were dug out of store, refurbished and set into action again. Anything, it seemed would sell. From 1945 to 1948, the best-selling Chevrolets were modified 1942 models. So were the Fords, and so were the Plymouths.

Most of the car-makers recovered rapidly from their military efforts and began building cars again during the autumn of 1945. Seventeen marques — with Ford and Chevrolet at the pinnacle and Crosley at the bottom — closed down in 1942, and the same 17 reopened for business in 1945. It looked like business-as-usual; if you had slept for four years you would have noticed no change.

But then, for 1946, two new marque names entered the fray: Frazer and Kaiser. These cars were the twin brainchilds, logically enough, of Joe Frazer and Henry J Kaiser, the first already renowned in the automobile industry, the other a ship-building tycoon. They took over the redundant Ford bomber aircraft assembly plant at Willow Run, near Detroit, and set out to challenge the Detroit 'establishment' at its own game. Also, Tucker said it was going to build lots of sleek new cars, but the project died at birth.

That, in fact, was the last upheaval in the *status quo*, for the established United States automobile industry had shrugged off these latecomers by 1955. It also quietly killed off several marques of its own in the decade which followed, though others were launched in their place.

In the last pre-war year, the Americans had produced 3,760,000 private cars, with General Motors right on top of the heap, taking a 48 per cent market share, Chrysler behind them with 23.4 per cent, and Ford third with 18.3 per cent.

LEFT: *Throughout the post-war expansion, Cadillac had Detroit's best-equipped and best selling luxury range of cars. All the cars had powerful V8 engines, this being a 1953 Coupe de Ville model.*

BELOW: *Madison Avenue's advertising genius at its best – this is a promotional still for a late-1950s Cadillac.*

RIGHT: *Cadillacs looked better in some years than others. This 1952 example had a very dumpy roof line, but that didn't stop the US citizen queueing up to buy.*

The largest of the 'independents' was Studebaker (3.2 per cent), and others – Nash, Hudson, Packard and Willys-Overland – were scratching around for sales to keep themselves alive. Except that Ford, led by Henry Ford II instead of his grandfather Henry Ford I, rapidly overtook Chrysler, this was the pattern of the post-war industry as well.

The American automobile industry recovered remarkably quickly, and by 1950 was making no fewer than six million cars a year. All the first generation of post-war cars were on sale, and Chevrolet alone was building 1.5 million cars annually. In the 1940s Cadillac and Oldsmobile introduced efficient new V8s, and although General Motors were world-leaders with automatic transmission, at the end of that decade several other groups were about to emulate them.

In the 1950s, American cars grew larger, faster, heavier, and ever more self-indulgent. Detroit complacently built the cars it thought Americans wanted, for exports were not needed, and there was increasing prosperity throughout the land. This was the period of styling excess – such as the Cadillac 'tail-fin' craze created by Harley Earl – of vastly powerful V8 engines, and of seemingly limitless choice of body styles, engines, transmissions and options.

Annual production stayed about the same, and by 1960 there were 19 different marques on sale. On the way, though, Kaiser, Frazer, Nash, Hudson, Packard and Crosley had gone, with Rambler, Checker, Imperial, Edsel and Continental on the market instead.

LEFT: *Checker's famous 'Yellow Cab' became an integral part of the New York scene in the 1960s.*

OPPOSITE BELOW: *A 1957 Chrysler De Soto.*

BELOW: *A 1950s Lincoln, a rival to the Cadillac.*

BOTTOM: *Lee Iacocca inspired the birth of Lincoln's Continental Mk 3 in 1968.*

ABOVE: *In the mid 1960s Chevrolet was America's best selling car and the Impala its most familiar range. This was a 1964 Convertible, one of nearly 900,000 Impalas built in that year. Prices started at about $3,000.*

LEFT: *Ford's Mustang, launched in April 1964, appealed so much to young buyers that the first million were sold in less than two years. The best way to go cruisin' was to have a convertible, like this 1966 example.*

RIGHT: *The Pontiac Firebird (this is a Trans Am) was developed by GM to fight the Ford Mustang. All used the same formula — four seats, open or closed bodies, and hundreds of options.*

During the 1960s, annual sales rocketed to over eight million. A wave of compact cars (Ford Falcon and Chevrolet Corvair, for example) was followed by the sporting new Ford Mustang and the Pontiac GTO. Mergers and shutdowns saw the end of the Studebaker and De Soto. Seven-liter V8 engines with 425 hp advertised outputs (however optimistically measured) were on sale, and sheer size was obviously considered more important than efficiency.

In the early 1970s the gradual expansion continued, until 9.7 million cars were produced in 1973. By this time new legislation from Capitol Hill had begun to hit hard at the carmakers, who were forced to clean up and de-tune their engines, to add much safety equipment, and to add monstrous crashproof bumpers. But the Yom Kippur War of 1973, and the huge rise of oil prices that followed, hit even harder. By the end of the 1970s, not only were car sales down by millions, but the car-makers were having to produce radically smaller cars to meet demanding new government fuel-consumption targets.

In 1982, only five million cars were built in the United States, and it would be several years before the recovery was nearly complete. In retrospect, that near-10-million year of 1973 now looks like a bygone age.

LEFT: *Ford's Pinto, announced in 1970 a scaled-down Ford.*

BELOW: *A Dodge 'black-and-white' (police car) on a highway patrol.*

Middle-East Pressure

The 1970s oil price explosion

I N October 1973, war broke out once again between Israel and its Arab neighbors. The result of this was not only a military defeat for the Arabs but an upheaval in the oil price structure. Driving a car would never be as cheap again.

The first crude oil wells had been dug in the United States in the 1870s, and the vast reserves under the sands of the Middle East had been discovered and exploited between the wars. In the 1950s and 1960s, there always seemed to be a huge surplus of supply over demand which kept prices well down. Naturally the automobile industry was happy about this, but the oil-producing countries were not.

All was well as long as America could produce more oil than it needed and export the balance. By the end of the 1960s, however, the demand for oil (as gasoline, diesel fuel, and a raw material for the plastics industry) had increased so

ABOVE: *As a result of the Suez war of 1973, petrol became scarce. Gas stations often ran out.*

BELOW: *At various times during 1973-74, when rationing was rumoured, there were long queues.*

much that, for the first time, the United States had to start importing oil from abroad. The balance of power – literally, for crude oil was liquid power waiting to be refined – had shifted in favor of the Arab states.

When gasoline was cheap and plentiful, car-makers did not worry too much about fuel-efficiency or weight savings. Every year, it seemed, cars got larger, heavier, more powerful and more thirsty. In America, for instance, it was normal for a car to have more than 300hp, to weigh more than 4000 pounds and to achieve little more than 10 miles per gallon.

In the meantime, the Arabs had come to own more than half of the world's known oil reserves. They also set up the Organization of Petroleum Exporting Countries (OPEC) in an attempt to square up to the oil barons, and to control –

and if possible increase – their selling prices. By 1973, when crude prices had already been pushed up by a few cents a gallon (because of the United States' dominance, prices were always quoted in American currency), it looked as if there was less then 20 years' supply still in the ground.

OPEC was already flexing its muscles, ready to impose a large price rise, when the October 1973 war broke out. OPEC then also decided to use oil as a political weapon. Countries deemed to have helped Israel were denied supplies for a time, while all others suddenly had to pay no less than four times as much for their oil as they had previously done. The impact of this pressure was enormous – and there was no way around it. Other oil producers, recognizing a good profit when it was offered, also raised their prices to suit.

RIGHT: *Soaring oil prices led to the development of new small-car diesel engines. VW's small four-cylinder unit, used successfully in the Golf, set new trends right across Europe.*

BELOW: *In 1971, a Cadillac Brougham like this was ideal for North American conditions, but by 1974 it suddenly looked heavy and thirsty.*

RIGHT: *From 1974 onward 'gas guzzlers' like this 4700lb, 365hp, 12mpg Lincoln Continental lost their appeal. 'Downsizing' was the only answer – though it took time.*

BELOW RIGHT: *Mercedes-Benz had always made economical diesel-engined cars but from 1974 they became more popular. especially in the USA. This is a five-cylinder 300D model.*

In the short term, gasoline prices rose sharply (in Britain they doubled within a year, and there were similar movements all around the world), and drivers used their cars more sparingly than before.

In the medium term, car-makers raced to make their cars more economical and to tailor them to the fuel-saving legislation that was rushed through in most countries.

In the long term, the search for alternative sources of energy and non-OPEC supplies of crude oil intensified. In general, new cars were designed to be smaller, lighter and more fuel-efficient, and with more slippery aerodynamic shapes. But it all took time and only in the late 1980s was the full impact obvious.

The OPEC countries had a bigger hold on some countries than on others. Japan, for instance, had no crude oil supplies of its own, and so was totally reliant on supplies from the Middle East. The United States made every effort to balance supply with demand and eventually cut its reliance on imported oil. Ample supplies of crude oil had been located under the North Sea, around the British Isles, and the higher prices now made it feasible to extract it for worldwide use.

For the next few years, OPEC lorded it over the world's car owners, gathering, and spending, huge amounts of money to develop their countries. Jokes about Arabs abandoning their Cadillacs when the ashtrays were full, no longer seemed funny to hard-pressed drivers, who were forced to observe lower speed limits and put up with the worldwide inflation that developed.

Yet more Middle East traumas, centered on Iran in 1979, led to another supply crisis in 1979 and a redoubling of the price of crude oil. By 1980 crude cost 10 times what it had cost in 1972. Gasoline prices shot up again – in Britain a gallon cost £1.20 in 1979, compared to 32p in 1970.

In the 1980s, however, the balance shifted again. Many alternative oil supplies had been found, extracted and put on sale – notably from Alaska and the Far East – and by 1984 the OPEC share was down to less than one-third of the world market. Nevertheless, prices and production stayed stubbornly high until 1985, when an oil glut caused prices to collapse.

Within months, benchmark prices slumped from more than $30 dollars a barrel (which is 35 gallons) to $10 or $11, OPEC countries' economies were shaken, and a decade of price war was over. Although prices recovered later, this was only done by restricting production in order to balance supply to demand.

Such price hikes will probably not occur again unless one entire region fof the world stops producing crude for long periods. Unless, that is, there is further fighting in the most productive areas. . .

Cleaning Up Exhausts

The impossible takes a little time

IF it had not been for the peculiar climatic conditions of the Los Angeles basin, there might have been no serious control of car engine exhaust systems until the 1970s. However, by the 1960s, as North America's most motorized city, Los Angeles began to suffer from serious smog problems. The cause, as researchers later confirmed, was the conversion of many different emissions into a foul-smelling fog. But the automobile got most of the blame.

When the car was first invented in the 1880s, it was enough of a miracle that an explosion of a gasoline/air mix-ture could be harnessed to produce power, and no thought was given to what was in the exhaust gases. For some years, in any case, there were so few cars, producing so little power, that their exhausts did not present a problem. The odors emitted by the automobile's rival, the horse, and the deposits left behind in its passing, were equally noxious.

Once cars began to dominate city streets, and the phrase 'traffic jam' became known, exhaust pollution became a problem. Quite simply, the burning of gasoline with air produced several exhaust gases. The least harmful of these was steam, but the obnoxious compounds included oxides of nitrogen, carbon monoxide (which is potentially lethal, if breathed in sufficient concentration), and unburned hydrocarbons. These all had objectionable smells, could harm plant life, and were suspected to be harmful to people and animals who breathed them.

They were doubly dangerous because they were invisible. The smoke from a diesel engine, especially when it was cold, was obvious, and of course it tasted awful and left a deposit, but it was no more harmful, and you could tell it was there.

By the 1960s, the pollution problem was becoming serious in many cities, though not at all noticeable in the country-side. The Los Angeles problem was made worse by what is known as photochemical reaction, where the hot Californian sunshine interacted with the nitrogen and hydrocarbon compounds to form a brown fog. The fact that electric power stations and aircraft all added to the chemical soup went largely unmentioned. The automobile was marked out as the prime culprit.

The first legal steps to control, and eventually to reduce dramatically, the emissions from car engines, were made in the United States. In the early 1960s all engines had to have closed-circuit crankcase breathing (where oil fumes were fed back into the inlet manifolds), but by the late 1960s legislation required all the emissions to be drastically reduced. Stringent high-mileage endurance tests had to be carried out by all car-makers to prove that their engines would not lose their tune as they grew old.

LEFT: *To cut down on pollution and to protect the environment unleaded fuel was introduced into the USA in the 1970s and Europe in the 1980s.*

BELOW: *Getting the last pollutants out of car exhausts was difficult and expensive, and could only be achieved by using exhaust catalysts.*

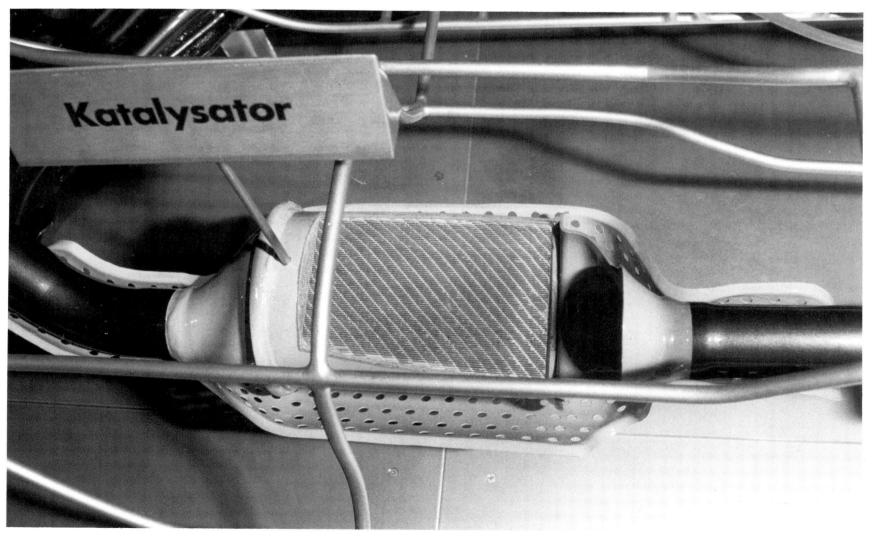

During the 1960s, American 'gas guzzlers' had their emissions reduced by two-thirds, but laws newly passed in 1967 required levels to be reduced by 95 per cent over a 10-year period, or in other words, almost eliminated. It looked like an impossible target – the legislators knew this, and the engineers said so – but sensational advances were made in the 1970s to meet the progressively more demanding levels applied from year to year. One respected chief engineer said, quite bluntly: 'They are asking us to exhaust cleaner air than we take in!'

At first, legislative limits could be met with carefully reset carburation and some changes to engine combustion; some engines were more efficient, and easier to modify, than others. The next step required air injection into exhaust manifolds (to help complete the combustion process), or for some of the exhaust to be recirculated into the engine itself.

Then, in early 1970s, companies like Honda began to introduce completely new engine designs with multi-valve heads, and with every attention given to complete combustion, rather than to horsepower. When the first energy crisis erupted in 1973-74, it suddenly became necessary to produce more economical engines, but the irony was that exhaust emission control tended to produce less efficient engines.

After the United States, other countries – notably Japan and Sweden – rushed to pass similar pollution-reducing laws, and before long other developed nations in Europe, Australasia and elsewhere joined in. Although most countries set different standards from their neighbors, car-makers generally were faced with the same problem all over the globe.

There was a further complication. Pressure from environmentalists (based on statistical evidence that is by no means conclusive) dictated the gradual reduction of lead additive in petrol. This automatically meant that octane ratings were reduced and that engine efficiency dropped yet again.

One result, therefore, was that the car-makers were backed into a very difficult position. On the one hand they had to produce more fuel-efficient cars (to meet both public demand and new legislation), while on the other they had to produce cars with clean exhausts which they knew to be less efficient. In America, the Clean Air Act had a lot to answer for. Fortunately, the development of catalysers (devices fitted into the exhaust systems to 'scrub' noxious compounds out of the gases) helped bring down emissions to their current levels.

There were three obvious results. One was that car engines became much more complex and expensive to build. Another was that the use of catalysers also forced up prices. The third was that cars tended to become less powerful, and usually smaller, so that they could retain the same performance as their predecessors.

In a generation, though, development engineers have very nearly achieved the impossible. Pollution levels have been reduced and city centers are more pleasant places to live in. But the limits have now been reached and the law-makers acknowledge this. Unless a completely new type of car engine is developed, there will always be exhaust gases. We must learn to live with them.

RIGHT: *In spite of safety and emission legislation, there was still fun to be had on the open road. The 1980s-style Ford Mustangs were better, if not faster, than any of their ancestors.*

ABOVE RIGHT: *MG could not 'de-tox' its V8 engined MGB to meet USA targets, so the 125mph, MGB GT V8s did not cross the Atlantic to the States.*

OPPOSITE: *With the numbers of cars increasing on the world's roads, every effort had to be made to reduce exhaust pollution. America's car makers made great strides in complying with the new laws.*

Technology to the Fore

Turbocharging and four-wheel drive.
Whatever next?

DO you remember when cars were simple, and many a repair job was tackled in the garage, or even at the kerbside? On the other hand, do you remember when you had to change oils, and get the car serviced, at 1000-mile intervals? Truly, they don't build cars like that any more!

Of course, there have always been simple cars and complicated cars, cheap cars and expensive cars, small and large cars. It is only in the last 20 years or so, however, that advanced and complex features have found their way into millions of family cars.

In the 1950s and 1960s, many family sedans had front engines, real-wheel-drive, independent front suspension and beam axle rear suspension. Even today, and especially in the United States and Canada, there are still many such new cars remain in existence today. But they are no longer in the majority.

By the 1960s, many small cars either had front engines and front-wheel-drive, or rear engines and rear-wheel-drive. Front-wheel-drive spread rapidly thereafter, to larger and more powerful cars, and was often linked with the use of independent rear suspension.

In the last decade, however, there has been a rush of new technology, which makes ordinary cars more exciting, and fast cars simply sensational. The innovations of the 1970s had become normal by the late 1980s.

Bugatti built a four-wheel-drive racing car in 1932 and the Jeep made the layout famous during World War II, but the world's first production 4×4 passenger car was the Jensen FF built in 1966. The Jensen was expensive and tricky to maintain; indeed, four-wheel-drive for the masses was some way off.

The advantages of four-wheel-drive were obvious. It gave better-balanced handling, and a good deal more grip, than any 'conventional' two-wheel-drive car. In icy conditions, or on steep slippery hills, there was a definite advantage. The only drawbacks were the extra weight, the added complication and the cost involved.

Audi, of West Germany, produced the very fast four-wheel-drive Quattro in 1980, and gradually adopted the same system for its other cars. Technically it was not ideal at first, but later cars were thoroughly sophisticated.

The Quattro's example sparked off a host of other 4×4s, some fast and glossy like the latest Mercedes-Benz models, some as cheap and cheerful as the Fiat Panda 4×4. In the middle, there were versatile 4×4 models from Ford (Sierra and Scorpio), Lancia (Delta and Prisma), and Subaru.

As sales increase, costs go down. Modern 4×4 installations are compact and relatively simple. Before long, it seems, every 'advanced' manufacturer will have at least one such car in its range.

BELOW: *Ford's 1986 Sierra RS Cosworth had a 16-valve turbocharged 2-liter engine.*

OPPOSITE: *Audi's Quattro was the first of the 1980s generation of four-wheel-drive cars.*

LEFT: *This was the first innovative Oldsmobile for many years – the V8-engined, front-wheel-drive Toronado. A year later a similar Cadillac was on sale.*

ABOVE: *The latest, best and most economical automatic transmissions have four forward speeds, and an 'overdrive' top gear, like this Ford A4LD design.*

In the old days, car engines sometimes had mechanically driven compressors, called superchargers, to force in more air and help produce more power; these needed power to drive them, and the result was only partially successful. The turbocharger has now virtually replaced supercharging. Because this has a turbine wheel driven by exhaust gases, which itself drives the compressor, there is 'free power' – and, potentially, a great deal of it. Effectively, a turbocharger makes a small engine larger: when Saab produced the 2-liter Turbo model, they said it was equivalent to a normally aspirated 3-liter.

There is nothing new about turbochargers. They were first developed for aircraft and then found a home in truck engines. The world's first production turbo car was a Chevrolet Corvair in 1962, the first European application was the BMW2002 Turbo of 1973, but the first two quantity-production cars were the Porsche 911 Turbo and Saab Turbo models.

Once engineers had discovered ways of controlling the boost and minimizing 'turbo-lag' (that is the pause between flooring the throttle and the time the extra boost becomes available), dozens of turbocharged models were put on sale. The ultimate seal of approval was to come from Rolls-Royce, when they announced the Bentley Mulsanne Turbo in 1982.

If you hit the brakes too hard on a slippery surface, the wheels lock, the tires lose their grip, and the car may be flung into a spin. A car is safest of all when the wheels never lock at all; antilock braking makes driving on slippery surfaces so much easier.

Aircraft in World War II had crude antilock sensors on the wheels, as did the Jensen FF of the 1960s, but it was not until the 1980s that modern electronics made systems smaller, cheaper and more sophisticated. A West German system, called ABS (Antilock Braking System) was introduced on BMW and Mercedes-Benz cars, then adopted by Ford. This and rival installations are now found as standard on many mass-produced cars.

RIGHT: *Jaguar's new XJ6 took six years to develop, and went on sale in 1986 to widespread critical acclaim. The specification is packed with advanced electronics, the car more refined than any of its ancestors.*

BELOW: *The Ferrari Testarossa has a 390hp flat-12 engine mounted behind the seats, a five-speed gearbox, all-independent suspension, and a 180mph top speed. A peerless super car for the late 1980s.*

It took many years for designers to produce reliable and efficient carburetors, but until World War II there was no alternative. During that conflict, fighter aircraft sometimes needed to fly upside down without stalling the engine, it was then that fuel injection was developed to make this possible.

For cars, FI (or PI for petrol injection) was first found in Grand Prix racers like the 1954 Mercedes-Benz W196, next on production cars from Chevrolet, Maserati, Peugeot and Triumph, but not on mass-produced cars until the 1970s.

Since then Bosch of West Germany have dominated the scene, with their injection systems on cars as patrician as the Rolls-Royce Silver Spirit, as small as the Peugeot 205GTi,

TOP: *Britain's most complex and carefully-built car is the Rolls-Royce Silver Spirit.*

ABOVE: *Mazda's RX7 combines a fine chassis and good aerodynamics with a modern Wankel-type engine.*

and as exotic as the current turbocharged Formula 1 cars. Fuel-injection systems are now used on cars built in most continents, not only giving better fuel control and more power, but better exhaust emission characteristics too. After turbocharging and four-wheel-drive, one wonders what will be produced next . . .

Changing the Shape of Motoring

The aerodynamics revolution

WHEN fuel was cheap, performance was limited and the roads were empty, no one worried much about the shape of cars. Early cars were not so much styled as engineered, and were in any case descended from the carriages towed by horses. It was not until man started driving open cars at speeds above 50mph and felt the wind tugging at his face, that he realized a great deal of drag was being created.

It was the same story with aircraft. The first 'string bags' buffeted their way across the skies without a thought for the drag they suffered. It was not until engine power and performance rose that consideration was given to the shape of the machinery.

It became obvious that aerodynamic drag rose rapidly as speeds built up; in fact, if one doubles the speed, drag rises four times. The total drag of a car is governed by the speed, the frontal area of the car, and something known as the drag coefficient (Cd). To make a new car more 'slippery,' it helps to reduce the frontal area, but it also helps to have a low Cd. If the air has a hard time getting past the car, under it, or along the flanks, there is a lot of drag and a high Cd; a smooth car, on the other hand, offering little resistance, has a lower Cd.

Cars followed aircraft trends, but several years later. When World War II broke out, most aircraft were already streamlined, but many cars still had separately mounted headlamps, bumps, bulges, running boards and other hang-on items.

In the 1950s and 1960s, all newly designed cars were given more rounded body styles, with relatively smoother noses, and these presented less resistance to the air. In almost every case, however, style took precedence over aerodynamic efficiency. These, at least, were more effective than between-wars attempts at 'streamlining,' where cars tended to have smooth tails but bluff front ends. Since most such cars had massive vertical noses, the air still had to work hard to get around the sides and away to the rear.

Nowadays we talk of Cd figures below 0.30 for production sedans, but a great deal has recently been learned. Previously, Cd figures stayed obstinately high unless a stylist had made an inspired stab at the right sort of shape.

A 1920s Bugatti Grand Prix car had a Cd of 0.74, an average 1950s sedan would have a Cd of 0.55 or worse, while even the famous 'aerodynamic' Jaguar D-Type racing sports car had a Cd of 0.50. The Jowett Javelin's Cd was 0.41, whereas the advanced Citroën DS19 of 1955 recorded 0.38.

The incentive to produce low-drag cars came in the 1970s, as cruising speeds rose and the cost of fuel leaped alarmingly. Designers have been very successful in their endeavors, for an 'average' Cd figure in the 1970s was 0.40/0.44, while a modern car introduced in the late 1980s tends to have a Cd of 0.30 or even less.

How is it done? There is much more to achieving good aerodynamics than merely producing a smooth outside shape. The underside of the car has be as smooth as possible, all the air intakes and exits have to be in the right place, and the flow of air into, around, and out of the engine bay has to be very carefully managed indeed.

OPPOSITE ABOVE:*Sports cars like this 1936-style Jaguar SS100 looked magnificent but had awful aerodynamics. The front encouraged lift and to reach 100mph was something of a miracle.*

OPPOSITE: *Although many people hated the looks of the mid 1930s Chrysler and De Soto Airflow models, it was a praiseworthy attempt to smooth a car's lines to reduce the drag and improve performance and fuel economy.*

ABOVE: *When Mercedes-Benz produced the W196 sports car for racing in 1955, the aerodynamics were carefully considered. Headlamps were faired in, exhaust pipes were sited in a 'dead' area, and for Le Mans there was a moveable air brake mounted behind the cockpit.*

There are great difficulties to be solved:

Brakes get too hot if they do not get enough air to cool them – but too much air causes drag.

An engine cooling radiator needs lots of air to keep temperatures in check; too much causes drag, too little causes overheating.

A smooth underside lowers drag, but may encourage the engine, drive train and exhaust system to overheat.

The ideal shape for aerodynamics may be wrong for the running gear – and the people – to be fitted inside.

The ideal shape for straight-line speed may be very unstable in a side-wind.

The stability may change as the speed rises, due to a change in the position of what is known as the 'center of pressure.'

The body shape might begin to generate lift as speeds rise, in just the same way as an aircraft wing lifts the airplane off the runway.

The world's designers soon found that they had to investigate and eliminate all these problems in controlled conditions, which meant testing in specially developed wind-tunnels. Some companies still have no tunnel of their own, which sometimes shows up in the cars they build. Others now have so much knowledge of aerodynamics that their specialists can look at a rival's car, tot up the features that matter, and predict a drag coefficient accurately before even testing it.

An ideal teardrop shape might have a Cd of only 0.05, but it is not really practical to make a car – complete with wheels, cooling ducts, doors, glass, bumpers, mirrors and an exposed underbody – to have a Cd of less than 0.30. Even then, an 'ideal' shape is difficult to devise, which explains why so many cars have under-bumper front spoilers (to stop air from getting under the car), and rear spoilers (to kill the high-speed lift).

Great advances have been made in the last 10 years. Will there be further improvements before the year 2000?

BELOW: *The Plymouth Roadrunner Superbird of 1970 used a sharp nose, and a rear 'wing' to improve aerodynamic shape.*

RIGHT: *The Citroen DS19 caused a sensation when launched in 1955.*

FAR RIGHT: *Audi's new 100 is an exceptionally good aerodynamic design.*

RIGHT: *The British MG Metro 6R4, with added front and rear spoilers to produce downforce, enabling better roadholding at high speeds.*

BELOW: *Ford's RS200 developed positive down force at high speeds, and scooped air over the roof to cool the turbocharged air.*

The Porsche Tradition

There's no substitute for technology!

O NE name above all others has been famous in the world of the automobile throughout the twentieth century: Porsche. It was Dr Ferdinand Porsche himself who towered above so many other great designers between the two World Wars, but it is the company bearing his name which has meant so much in recent years.

Porsche's design bureau sold its expertise to clients far and wide in the 1930s. At the end of World War II it was evacuated to Gmünd, in Austria. There, as chaos gradually gave way to peacetime austerity, the company began to find its feet again, at first with work on tractors, then in designing a new Grand Prix car for Cisitalia, and finally in the development of its own Porsche sports car. Once true prosperity began to return to Western Europe and the business moved back to Stuttgart in West Germany, Porsche's design expertise flourished.

Although Dr Porsche himself died in 1951, his son Ferry, and son-in-law Anton Piëch, remained true to his ideals, and the company built up an amazing reputation in the world's automobile industry. Even in the 1930s and 1940s the Porsche design bureau had designed a wide variety of successful machines. What could be more different, for instance, than a VW Beetle 'people's car,' a super-heavy armored fighting vehicle and an Auto-Union Grand Prix car?

Porsche's commercial future was underpinned from 1949 by a royalty agreement with VW. For every machine in the Beetle family that was built, Porsche was contracted to receive 5DM. At the time this represented about 40p, or about $1.00, and as VW production built up in the 1950s and 1960s it gave Porsche the financial stability it needed. Not only could it continue building its own sports cars and designing new models, but it could carry on inventing new features and selling them to the world at large. There was no shortage of customers. In the 1930s, most car-makers had been independent, and had in any case shied away from doing deals with Hitler's Germany, but none of them had underestimated the importance of Porsche inventions like the Beetle's torsion-bar independent front suspension, the ZF-type limited-slip differential, and what has now commonly become known as 'Porsche' synchromesh.

In the 1950s, Porsche rapidly began to run out of space in its Stuttgart-Zuffenhausen factories. Accordingly in 1960, the company bought a large parcel of ground near Weissach, west of Stuttgart, where construction of a large research and development center, proving ground and test track began. By the late 1970s, when the consulting side of Porche's business was as valuable as its car-making activity, more than 1500 people (out of total workforce of 5000) were based at Weissach.

ABOVE: *In 1947, Porsche began designing a new GP car for Cisitalia. This had a 12-cylinder engine mounted behind the driver, while provision was made for the advantage of four-wheel-drive being added at a later date.*

RIGHT: *Porsche's first production car was the Type 356 sports model, built from 1949 to 1964 in coupe, hard top, convertible, or Speedster guise. All had rear-mounted air-cooled engines.*

For its own purposes, Porsche beavered away at new air-cooled engine designs, like the four-cam Carrera unit of the 1960s, the flat-eight Grand Prix 1.5-liter that followed it, and eventually the famous flat-six unit found in the Porsche 911 family. The irony was that although Porsche's research and development was always diligent and thorough, it refused to move away from its own superficially archaic car designs – rear engines, swing-axle rear suspension and air-cooling all persisted at Porsche for years after they had been abandoned elsewhere.

In the 1960s the company was drawn into cooperative car design ventures. Over the years, dozens of prototypes were built for VW, though few ever saw the light of day. At the end

ABOVE: *The fabulous air-cooled flat-12 Type 917 racing sports Porsche, which won the World Championship in 1970 and 1971.*

LEFT: *The Porsche which everyone knows – the 911 model, introduced in 1963 and still selling in the late 1980s. All have rear-mounted air-cooled six-cylinder engines.*

RIGHT: *A 1970 model of the famed 911, incorporating a number of modifications including a lengthened wheelbase and wider rear track.*

of the decade, however, the rather awkwardly styled mid-engined VW-Porsche 914 model was announced – a Porsche-designed car originally meant to have been built solely by VW itself.

By that time, too, Porsche was heavily involved in a Beetle-replacement for VW, the mid-engined water-cooled EA266 project, but after this was abruptly cancelled in 1971 Weissach needed more work, fast. It was at this juncture that Porsche designed the front-engined 924 for Audi. At the last minute Audi withdrew, the car took on a pure 'Porsche' name, but it was still assembled in an Audi factory!

Porsche's designers were incredibly inventive and its development engineers resourceful, so perhaps we should not be amazed to consider the variety of projects to come out of Weissach in the recent past. On the one hand there were the fabulous air-cooled flat-12 and flat-16 racing engines for the equally outstanding 917 racing sports car; on the other there was the development of a completely new range of engines for the Spanish car-maker SEAT. Yet again, there was the design and development of the V6 turbocharged TAG engine used in the all-conquering McLaren Formula 1 cars, and there was the painstaking work done to produce very longlife corrosion-free body structures.

Nor was there any reluctance to innovate. Porsche was the first European car-maker to put a turbocharged engine into

ABOVE: *In the 1970s Porsche built up its Weissach research center and carried out much work for other clients. The Spanish concern SEAT hired Porsche to design a new range of engines for the Ibiza hatchback family.*

RIGHT: *In the mid-1970s, Porsche turned to making cars with water-cooled front-mounted engines. The flagship of the range was the V8-engined 928. This is a 1985 model 928S2.*

serious long-term production. Its latest 956-type turbocharged engines had air-cooled cylinder barrels but water-cooled cylinder heads. In the 1960s its production mainstay had been a car with an air-cooled engine at the rear; for the 1980s this philosophy had changed, to embrace water-cooled engines mounted at the front and driving the rear wheels. Then, of course, there was the extremely complex four-wheel-drive installation of the 959 Group B project, work on entirely new cars for Iron Curtain manufacturers, and. . .

At which point, Porsche's security curtain comes down, for the moment. In the future, though, you can be certain that more innovation, more contract work and more great ideas will continue to pour out of Weissach. There is, after all, a great Porsche tradition to be upheld.

RIGHT INSET: *Although based on the 911's layout, the 959 was a limited-production competition car with four-wheel-drive, and water-cooled cylinder heads.*

LEFT INSET: *By the mid-1980s the basic 911 had been turbocharged, given a new nose, extra engine air inlets, and looked just like a road-going race car.*

BELOW: *Originally designed for VW, this became the 924, Porsche's best-selling car of the 1970s and 1980s. For 1986 it had a Porsche engine, and was called the 924S.*

Downsizing the Monsters

Facing up to economic reality in the USA

TWENTY years ago, the roads of North America were full of enormous cars. But not any more. Since then, American cars have been shrinking, and the change is not yet complete. The vast old-style cars are now described as 'dinosaurs,' and although a few very large cars are still being made, the day of the North American 'land-cruiser' has gone for good.

How and why did this happen? In summary: after World War II American cars continued to grow as the nation's prosperity increased and the price of raw materials and gasoline stayed low. The downturn came in the 1970s, and more obviously in the 1980s, as costs rose rapidly and gasoline needed to be conserved.

In the 1950s and 1960s there never seemed to be a need to make American cars as compact as possible. There was plenty of road space, thousands of miles of new highways to use, and a great deal of money to be spent. Large, powerful, heavy and thirsty V8 engines, backed by automatic transmissions, were normal. Every time a model was changed or facelifted, it seemed to get a bit longer, a bit wider, with more weight balanced by more power.

As an example, in 1950 the best-selling Chevrolet Skyline had a 92hp six-cylinder engine and weighed about 3100 pounds. In the 1960 the Bel Air had 135hp, with V8 options

up to 335hp, and weighed 3500 pounds. In 1970 Bel Airs and Impalas had V8 engines going up to 390hp and weighed about 3650 pounds. The same growth had occurred in every other American range of cars.

Detroit's bosses kept trying to stem the tide, but with little success. Usually they produced new lines of smaller cars, while allowing the existing cars to continue. Then the process started again, and the smaller cars got bigger, heavier and more powerful.

In 1959 there was a rush of new 'compacts' (Corvair, Falcon, Valiant), which soon led to 'super compacts' and 'intermediates' being produced. Then in the 1960s there was the relatively small-sized 'pony' car (Mustang, Camaro, Firebird), which also began to grow and to put on weight. General Motors and Ford usually led the way, with Chrysler and American Motors struggling to stay in touch.

In 1970 and 1971 the 'Big Two' tried again, with Ford announcing the 103-inch wheelbase Maverick, and then the tiny 94.2-inch wheelbase Pinto, while Chevrolet produced the 97-inch wheelbase Vega. That was just a sighting shot, for the need to 'downsize' was still a question of social responsibility rather than economic reality. Chrysler missed out, but American Motors cropped off one of their larger cars to produce the stubby Gremlin.

In the early 1970s, however, those economic pressures arrived with a vengeance. The fight to control pollution, conservation and rocketing oil prices (with the possibility of shortages in future years) led to reams of new legislation. Quite suddenly, vast cars were seen as wasteful and antisocial.

OPPOSITE ABOVE: *In 1960 Ford's Falcon was a 'compact,' which grew inexorably larger over the years. Ford later added the Maverick and Pinto lines to fill the gaps.*

OPPOSITE BELOW: *By the mid-1970s even the so-called 'personal' cars were very large indeed. These are the front-drive Cadillac Eldorados which weighed 5100lb.*

RIGHT, TOP TO BOTTOM: *A sequence showing the way the Pontiac Bonneville has shrunk over the years. The largest car was the new 1974 model, followed by the 'downsized' 1977 variety, the even smaller, squared-up 1982 version and finally the latest 1987 Bonneville. Weights have fallen from 4400lb in 1974 to 3300 in 1987.*

ABOVE: *A perfect example of a good car grown too large. This 1975 Cadillac Eldorado was 600lb heavier than the Eldorado of 1967, had a 6-inch longer wheelbase, and a 500ci rather than a 429ci V8 engine.*

LEFT: *For 1978, Plymouth took a bold step by introducing this European-designed Horizon as its base car. It had front-wheel-drive, a 105ci engine, and weighed only 2150lb.*

Market leader General Motors led the way and the rest made haste to follow. Even before the 1973/74 energy crisis erupted, GM had decided to downsize their cars, but it took three years to turn this plan into reality. The B-Body and C-Body models (cars like the full-size Chevrolets and the Oldsmobile Deltas) lost several inches in the wheelbase and up to 800 pounds in weight. In the years that followed, other ranges shrank too.

In the meantime, even smaller cars were 'taken over' from European and Japanese associate companies and sold in the United States. Ford began selling pint-sized front-drive Fiestas in 1977, while General Motors started building Chevrolet Chevettes in 1976. Chrysler produced the Plymouth Horizon (really a Chrysler/Simca Horizon) in 1978, while American Motors (AMC) added the grotesque Pacer to their model line-up.

At that time, the way to make cars smaller was to cut back on front and back overhangs, slim down the doors, and sometimes (without actually admitting it) make the passenger cabins a bit smaller. The next important step, first embraced by GM, was to give priority to passengers, and make engines and drive trains more compact.

The best way to do this was to adopt front-wheel-drive with transverse engines. The first GM cars in this style were the Chevrolet Citations of 1979, with four-cylinder or V6 engines. Ford, however, went one better, with a front-wheel-drive Escort of 1980, which was effectively an Americanized version of the new European Escort.

In the meantime, new United States legislation meant that all cars would have to get smaller – a lot smaller. New laws requiring a progressively higher Corporate Average Fuel Economy (CAFE) figure specified *average* fuel consumption figures of 21.6 (Imperial) miles per gallon by 1977, and no less than 33 (Imperial) miles per gallon by 1985. Failure to meet this would result in huge fines.

Marques like Rolls-Royce, which imported about 1000 cars a year, could afford to shrug off the new laws, but no American company could ignore them. It was obvious that the only answer, once again, was to make the cars progressively smaller, with smaller engines, and with higher fuel efficiency.

Everyone – managers, engineers and pundits alike – agreed that this eventually meant European-sized cars with front-wheel-drive were needed, and this is precisely what America got. General Motors decided to set up cooperative projects with the Japanese (several of their small mid-1980s

cars were pure Yokohama in design), to Americanize the new Opel Ascona/Vauxhall Cavalier as their corporate 'J-Car,' and to develop smaller front-drive versions of cars as diverse as the Cadillac Seville and the Pontiac Grand Am. Ford produced the Tempo and Taurus cars, while Chrysler introduced their versatile 'K' models. American Motors could not cope and rushed to the safe arms of Renault, to build modified Renault 9s and 11s in America.

By the late 1980s, the downsizing program was nearly complete, and on average engines were only about half as powerful as in 1970. What will be the next economic effect on Detroit?

OPPOSITE INSET: *Some downsizing strategies did not work. GM introduced a new corporate J-car, with front-wheel-drive, and called one version a Cadillac (the Cimarron). Few bought what was considered a bogus car.*

BELOW: *It was surprising that Pontiac ever gained corporate approval to build the mid-engined Fiero, a sports coupe inspired by the Fiat X1/9. Small, neat and nimble, it was, however, just right for the late 1980s.*

Let's All Hold Hands

The industry merges its resources

ARE you surprised to learn that some modern Volvos use VW or Renault engines? That a car called a Pontiac Le Mans is really an Opel Kadett built in Korea? That a Rover Sterling shares most of its engine, drive train and body structure with the Honda Legend? That the same basic structure went into the design of the Saab 9000, the Lancia Thema and the Fiat Croma?

If you did not know, do not be ashamed to admit it. The world's automobile industry is now a very complex business, for almost every company has links with another – commercially, financially or technically. Few of them would be able to survive unless they did.

BELOW: *Rover (Sterling) 800 and Honda Legend cars have different styling; top of the line cars share the same Honda engine.*

RIGHT: *The Rover 800 Series (Sterling in the USA) was a joint project between Austin-Rover in England and Japan's Honda.*

ABOVE: *Saab's 9000 uses its own unique type of 16-valve twin-cam engine, but has the same basic front-wheel-drive layout as the Lancia Thema and Fiat Croma models. The most powerful version has a 175hp output.*

LEFT: *The Lancia Thema of 1984 was the first of the jointly-conceived European 'Type 4' cars to be shown. It used Fiat engines, and had more in common with the Croma than the 9000.*

RIGHT: *The Fiat Croma was the third of the Type 4 cars to be launched, shares features with the Lancia and was to be joined by the other Type 4, the Alfa Romeo 164, in 1987.*

There is nothing new about mergers or the use of common parts. The world's biggest car corporation, General Motors, set the standard for everyone when it came into existence in 1908; famous names which joined together at that time included Cadillac, Chevrolet, Buick and Oldsmobile.

Even before World War II, other companies were getting together, trading their independence for security. Daimler joined with Benz in 1926, Morris took over Wolseley in 1926, Daimler annexed Lanchester in 1931, and before 1939 General Motors had bought up Vauxhall in England and Opel in Germany. Detroit's 'Big Three' corporations even began buying components from each other.

Until the 1960s, the 'urge to merge' was usually due to tycoons wanting to get bigger and more powerful; entire companies got together and individual identities were lost. In recent years there has been a much more basic reason. It has now become so expensive to design, and tool up for, new engines, drive trains and models, that few companies can

afford to do it on their own; nowadays they tackle joint design projects and share in the results, but otherwise stay aloof from one another.

Until the 1960s, cars were relatively simple. Car-makers either built their own products or bought them in from specialist suppliers. It was usual for them to build their own running gear, but quite a number went outside for bodies, or perhaps for specialist drive trains.

At this time, though, they began to learn from General Motors and Ford. Not only did these massive combines make sure that engines and drive trains were shared between makes and models, but sometimes even between countries. By the beginning of the 1970s, General Motors' Australian Holden cars had a lot in common with European Vauxhalls or Opels, Ford were building essentially the same cars in Britain and West Germany, while both had satellite plants assembling similar cars in South Africa and South America. Soon after this they forged financial links with Japanese

concerns – GM with Isuzu and Ford with Toyo Kogyo (who made Mazdas).

Then came the energy crisis, the rapid increase in gasoline prices and the worldwide inflation that followed. At the same time cars were becoming more complex and had to meet many more sets of regulations. Large corporations could cope with this, but the smaller 'independents' found it difficult to obtain the money for modifications and new models.

During the 1970s, therefore, almost every car-maker talked to every other one, desperately looking for ways to merge ideas without merging their business, looking for novelties which they could afford, and looking for ways to bring down costs.

The large corporations themselves, with worldwide interests, began to edge their way towards the 'world car.' General Motors' T-Car project – an Opel Kadett in West Germany, a Vauxhall Chevette in England, a Chevrolet Chevette in the United States, an Isuzu Gemini in Japan, and a different type of Chevrolet Chevette in Brazil – was a perfect example. Ford, for their part, introduced a front-drive Escort in Europe, and a similar but not identical Escort in the United States.

The independent companies did it differently. They soon found that they were happy to swap engines and drive trains – 'building blocks,' as they became known in automobile-industry jargon – while jealously guarding their individual body styles.

The 'arm's-length' link-up between Peugeot and Renault of France and Volvo of Sweden was typical. Each company wanted a new large-capacity engine, but none could find the resources to do this alone. By getting together and agreeing to share the investment, they were able to solve the problem. The PRV V6 engine was announced in 1974; it then found its way into several new cars in the next few years, and is still in production today. It even appeared in the ill-fated De Lorean sports car.

In Europe, in particular, things began to get very complicated. Ford of West Germany supplied engines to Saab. Volvo bought six-cylinder diesel engines from VW. Porsche bought automatic transmissions from Mercedes-Benz. British Leyland bought manual transmissions from VW. Fiat began a new small-car engine project with Peugeot (which was later cancelled). Renault provided small four-cylinder engines to Volvo-Holland.

RIGHT: *Although this 1985 car is called a Chevrolet Nova, it was derived from the Toyota Corolla, using Toyota engines and transmissions. Other modern Chevrolets are Suzuki and Isuzu based.*

OPPOSITE: *Austin-Rover's Maestro, announced in 1983, used VW manual and automatic transmissions.*

BELOW: *The smart French Renault 25 uses the same four-cylinder engines as Citroën and Peugeot and the same V6 engines as Peugeot and Volvo.*

Then the true joint projects came to the surface. The pan-European 'Type 4' project began on the basis of a common floor pan and suspensions for new Saab, Fiat and Lancia models; before long the similarities decreased, but Alfa Romeo joined in as well. British Leyland joined forces with Honda to produce the Ballade in Britain as the Triumph Acclaim; the next-generation Ballade was named Rover 200, but the result was the same. Alfa Romeo got together with Nissan to produce the ARNA model (Alfasud engine/drive train in a Nissan Cherry structure). More such schemes will surely surface soon.

In North America, the process is well advanced. The 1986 Chevrolet line started with a Sprint that was a modified Suzuki, the ancient Chevette, the Spectrum that was a modified Isuzu, and a Nova that was a modified Toyota. American Motors' Renault Alliance and Encore were modified Renault 9s and 11s.

The miracle is that companies like BMW and Mercedes-Benz are still independent.

BELOW: *Renault linked with AMC to produce the Alliance (USA) and the Renault 9 (France).*

RIGHT: *The Mazda 323 of 1980 was similar to the new front-drive Ford Escort.*

Acknowledgements

The publisher would like to thank Design 23 who designed this book, Melanie Earnshaw who did the picture research and Emma Callery who compiled the index. We would also like to thank the following agencies, institutions and individuals for supplying illustrations on the pages noted:
Audi-Volkswagen: pages 73 both, 75 inset, 76 top, 135 both, 149 inset
Autocar: pages 6, 17 below, 98, 114 top, 128 main, 129, 153, 165, 190/Nick Walsh: pages 160-161
Autosport: pages 114 below, 127 main
The Hulton Picture Company: pages 9 below, 12, 13 below, 15 below, 16 below, 36 top, 39, 40, 41, 49 top, 61 top, 77, 78-79, 92, 104, 112, 113 top, 116-117, 124-125, 147 both, 154
Henry Austin Clark Jr: pages 10 both, 13 top, 17 top, 18 below, 19 both, 23, 32 below, 36 below, 43 below, 44 both, 46-47 main picture, 55 top, 59 below, 63 inset, 88 below
Classic and Sportscar: pages 20-21, 22, 42, 64, 65 below, 91 inset, 93 top, 102 main, 136 main, 142 top/Nick Baldwin: page 28 below
John Colley/Haymarket Publishing: page 87 top
CW Editorial: pages 1, 21 below, 28 top, 34 below, 51 below and left, 56, 62-63, 69 top, 70 top, 95 below, 116 inset, 126, 127 inset, 137 below, 169 inset, 172, 173 top, 175, 176-177
Esso Petroleum: page 152
Fiat Auto (UK): page 101 below
Ford Motor Company: pages 35, 59 top, 66 top, 143 below, 155 below, 159 inset, 168-169
General Motors Corp: pages 60, 182 inset/Pontiac Motor Division: pages 81, 179 all four
GN Georgano: pages 34 top, 55 below, 65 top, 67, 69, 119, 166-167, 180-181, 188
William F Harrah Automobile Museum: pages 2-3, 14, 15 top, 16 top, 25, 27 both, 32 top, 43 top, 66 below
Haymarket Motoring Picture Library: pages 54 top, 87 below and top, 88 top, 113 below, 128, 136 inset, 137 top, 190 below
Haynes Publishing: pages 86, 166 top, 167 top, 176 inset
Imperial War Museum: page 75 inset
Jaguar: pages 118-119, 161 inset
Mike Key: page 142 below
Ludvigsen Library: pages 52-53, 93 below, 130-131, 132-133, 132 inset, 133 inset, 134, 140, 141, 146 below, 148-149, 162 top, 163
Mercedes-Benz: pages 8, 9 top, 48, 50 below, 51 top
Andrew Morland: pages 11 top, 31 below, 37 below, 49 below, 50 top, 56 below, 57 below, 68 below, 76 below, 83 top, 85 top, 97 top, 99 top, 105, 107 inset, 108 both, 109, 110-111, 11 inset, 141 inset
National Motor Museum, Beaulieu: pages 122-123, 124 inset, 145
Nissan UK: page 96
Porsche Cars Great Britain: pages 101 top, 170-171
Porsche Cars West Germany: pages 102 inset, 103 both
Quadrant Picture Library, Sutton, Surrey SM2 5AS: pages 11 below, 18 top, 20 below, 24 top, 27, 29, 37 top, 45, 47 inset, 54 below, 61 below, 68 top, 71 below, 84, 85 below, 87 middle, 97 top, 100, 101 below, 115, 138, 144 below, 150-151, 155 top, 156, 157, 158-159, 162 below, 174, 177 inset, 180 below, 182-183, 186, 187 top
Road and Track: pages 30, 146 top, 150 inset
Rolls-Royce Motor Cars: page 58
Richard Spiegelman: pages 24 below, 38, 57 top, 58 below, 79 inset, 80 both, 82 top, 82-83, 139, 140 inset, 144 top, 164 both
Toyota: page 99
What Car: pages 184, 185, 189 below
Nicky Wright/National Motor Museum, Beaulieu: pages 120-121, 121 inset